what will they say about you
when you are gone?

what will they say about you when you are gone?

CREATING A LIFE OF LEGACY

By Rabbi Daniel Cohen

Health Communications, Inc.
Deerfield Beach, Florida

www.hcibooks.com

Library of Congress Cataloging-in-Publication Data
is available through the Library of Congress

© 2016 Rabbi Daniel Cohen

ISBN-13: 978-07573-1951-8 (Paperback)
ISBN-10: 07573-1951-3 (Paperback)
ISBN-13: 978-07573-1952-5 (ePub)
ISBN-10: 07573-1952-1 (ePub)

Publisher: Health Communications, Inc.
        3201 S.W. 15th Street
        Deerfield Beach, FL 33442–8190

Cover and interior design and formatting by Lawna Patterson Oldfield
Cover photo © iStock by Getty Images

To
Dr. Noel Kriftcher—
Your soul continues
to soar!

CONTENTS

FOREWORD

I count Rabbi Daniel Cohen as one of my rabbis. As a lifelong member of Congregation Agudath Sholom in Stamford, Connecticut, and a close friend, I cherish our relationship and am honored to write this foreword to his new book, which embodies our highest aspirations.

Rabbi Cohen's path for creating a life of legacy can truly change each of us for the better and in turn improve the world. There's not one person alive who hasn't confronted his or her own mortality. Each of us, at some point, wakes up to the reality that our time on Earth is limited. We want to make the most of our potential and our time here. How do we lead our lives with a sense of urgency every day? How do we develop the courage to make choices not based on pressure but on principle? How do we create the sacred space to reflect on who we are and who we want to be so we can realize our innermost goals and dreams?

I am deeply fortunate to have been raised with parents in a community that was devoted to a faith that served as an anchor and inspiration for my commitment to public service, statesmanship, democracy, and unity. Over the years in my capacity as attorney general, US senator, and a candidate for vice president of the United

States, I've struggled to lead a principled life. Rabbi Cohen's focus on "Courageous Choices," in particular, is one that resonates deeply for me. We're all faced with moments when we must choose between the path of convenience or conviction. Rabbi Cohen's guidance for developing the moral fortitude to make courageous choices at every moment should inspire each of us every day.

Navigating life with clarity of purpose is not easy, but the rewards for doing so are enormous. Imagine for a moment if we lived our lives with the awareness of the eternal resonance of our words. Imagine if we harnessed all of our potential every day to improve ourselves, our families, our communities, and the world. Leading our lives in tune with this higher calling would also infuse our nation with greater progress, civility, unity, happiness, kindness, and honesty. The path to reverse engineering our lives is needed now more than ever. This book is a beacon of light and a touchstone for the timeless values of leading a purposeful life.

—*Senator Joseph Lieberman*

PREFACE

"Feed a man a fish,
you feed him for a night.
Teach a man to fish,
you feed him for a lifetime."

—Ancient Proverb

My father, Noel Kriftcher, passed away in March 2011 at the age of seventy-one following an eighteen-month battle with brain cancer. I think of him every day, bolstered by the lifetime of shared memories he helped create within our family. While I wish he had lived longer, I recognize how fortunate we are to have had him in our lives for the time we did, and for his belief that it was his calling to not forgo any opportunity for a teachable moment, the lessons that continue to profoundly influence so many. Many of the lessons I learned from my father in life—and, unfortunately, in death—have found a voice in this book. I couldn't be more grateful to my close, personal friend and spiritual beacon, Rabbi Cohen, for providing this forum for my father's legacy to remain alive and well. The residue of an inspired life lived!

In Yiddish, there is a word, *bashert*, which loosely translated means "meant to be." Indeed, it was *bashert* that I met Rabbi Cohen nearly a decade ago, just after he and his family moved to Stamford, Connecticut, but prior to my retirement at forty years old from a successful nearly twenty-year business career in order to pursue, on a full-time basis, teaching, coaching, and philanthropic work. The timing of when I met Rabbi Cohen allowed me to take him up on his offer to join him on a small group tour he was leading to Israel. I had never been to Israel before and thought it would be particularly special to invite my father to join me. The trip created a powerful bond among all of us, which provided tremendous comfort throughout the period of my father's illness, at his ultimate passing, and beyond. For this, too, I am immensely grateful to Rabbi Cohen.

A lifelong career educator who graduated from New York University at nineteen years old, ascended up through the ranks of New York City public education, and later directed a center for educational alliances and technology at NYU Polytechnic University in Brooklyn, my father was a champion of the role education could play in ensuring an overall level playing field. Devotions to family, faith, education, and athletics (primarily basketball) were his magnet and his anchor—and so, too, these have served as a magnet and anchor for my siblings and me. At his packed funeral, eulogies from family and friends emphasized the deep and powerful impact my father had on their lives. Following the funeral, a number of people remarked to me how the feelings expressed inspired them to want to be more impactful in their own lives. It is a sentiment Rabbi Cohen himself has heard many times over in his professional role. And it became the basis for "What Will They Say About You When You Are Gone?" Rabbi Cohen and my weekly "fireside chats" over the ensuing years have taught me much. Among other things, they have allowed me to reflect carefully on the lessons I learned from my father during his lifetime—wisdom that he imparted by his daily deeds more than his spoken words—and that he conveyed in small increments rather than one grand gesture. It is impossible to sum up pearls of wisdom that came my way over a forty-five-year span together. However, among those most impactful were:

- We are obliged to leave the world better than we found it.
- Find a way to contribute three "Ws" to any organization you are part of: wealth, wisdom, and work.
- Leadership means being the best of people some of the time but one of the people all of the time.
- Be proud of your heritage.
- The answer to the question "What do I make?" is not a monetary amount but rather that "I make people think, believe, and dream."
- Somewhere in Kenya a child is training, even (especially) when you're too tired to do so.
- In baseball, a player is neither out nor safe on his own; he's not anything until the umpire says what he is. Respect the call!
- Our role with children is to help them dream in color, even when in front of them is only black and white.

While he passed quickly, I believe my father lived the life by which he wanted to be remembered. I can only hope that the readers of this book will do the same. The time is short; the task is abundant. Godspeed.

—Brian S. Kriftcher
Stamford, Connecticut
July 2016

ACKNOWLEDGMENTS

I can't tell you how many times I cried while writing this book. Sometimes the tears were from sadness when reflecting on the fragility of life and sometimes they welled up from the intense personal struggle to find the time and space for everyone and everything. Most often, tears of joy emerged from sensing myself as a vessel for God. After finishing a section of the book, I'd turn upward toward my mother, of blessed memory, my muse, and thank her and God for almost magically enabling me to transform disparate thoughts into what I hope is a coherent, timeless, and captivating message. My mother lives with me every day, and her love shines forth in all I do. My father, he should live and be well, is my hero. Your lessons, your love, your modeling a life of purpose, resilience, gratitude, optimism, wisdom, and godliness pulsate in me every day. I can't thank you enough. I love you very much. To Savta Meryl, thank you for your encouragement, love, and wisdom. You're a blessing for Abba and our family.

The book you're holding in your hands is the expression of so many people, some of whom I can name and some whose names I'll never know. I've written this book in multiple venues. Overlooking Long Island Sound, Block Island, Vail, from my office in Stamford to Starbucks in Stamford and New Canaan, I encountered people whose words rested on my heart, and the stirrings became the written word. We're all intrinsically tied to one another. One ripple, one gesture, one word of wisdom can reverberate across time and space. I'm eternally grateful for all of the souls whose revealed sparks touched mine and ignited a fire in my heart.

I'm deeply grateful to the leadership and membership of Congregation Agudath Sholom in Stamford, Connecticut, for your support, friendship, love, and openness to sharing our journeys together and for your understanding of my need for personal renewal. My writing refreshes my soul, enables me to see life in more color, and deepens my rabbinate. Thank you so much.

From my students I've learned more. Thank you to everyone who has shared Torah, faith, and learning with me. Over the years, I more fully understand that God descends when two people engage in the study of Torah. Thank you for revealing new ideas and sparks in the world.

We all have a book inside us waiting to be written. I can't begin to express my deepest appreciation to the people who believed in me and unlocked the song in my soul. To Brian Kriftcher: Our souls are intertwined. From start to finish, your friendship, support, wisdom, encouragement, and excitement lifted me to new heights. Your father lives in me, and I'm forever grateful for our time and his everlasting legacy. Rich Vogel: You're a dream maker. Thank you for your unconditional love and never-ending support and wisdom. The question was never "if" but "how." To Nicole Williams, Jill Jacinto, Barbie Alpert, Joanne McCall, and Fred Giordano: From the branding, design, strategy, marketing, and book proposal, you intuited the holiness of reverse engineering your life. Thank you so much for merging your talent and passion with our purpose. To Rick Sapkin, Diane

Reed, Amy Venturi, Jay Kamlet, and Pastor Greg Doll: Your wisdom, time, and faith in me are invaluable, and I'm eternally grateful. God bless you all!

We can only fly with angels who carry us. Thank you to Bryan Mattimore and Ken Schwartz for your friendship, guidance, and leading me to Anne Marie O'Farrell, my agent. Anne Marie, you're the best! Although from different faiths, we share a kindred spirit, and I truly value your honesty, wisdom, and experience. I'm eternally indebted to HCI Books and their stellar team, including Allison Janse, Cathy Slovensky, Kim Weiss, and company.

I'm blessed with so many angels in my life who are sources of inspiration. Thank you to Rabbi J. J. Schachter, David Federman, David Schnall, Ken Schur, Rabbi Hayim Herring, Rabbi Daniel Estreicher, Ian Wishingrad, Martin Kasdan, Tom Gallagher, Gary Channer, Allison Josephs, Sandy Goldstein, Michael Friedman, Dr. Arlen and Audrey Lichter, Ruth Melman, Michael Opatowski, Aunt Sherri and Uncle Michael Umansky, Senator Joseph Lieberman, and to my siblings, Elie, Rachel, Joel, Marty, Ezra, Benyamin, and Chanie. Heartfelt thanks to Ron Howard, Rudy Giuliani, Chuck Leavell, Anne Curry, Steve Schwarzman, Tamir Goodman, David Harris, Dannel Malloy, and Mayim Bialik for your openness in sharing your life experiences and sources of inspiration.

The spirit of my grandparents, Harry and Claire Umansky and David and Johanna Cohen, and Diane's parents, Isaac and Ruth Jacobs, are woven into the book implicitly and live on in what I say, write, and do. May their memories be for a blessing.

To our daughters—Sara Malka, Michal, Adina, Elisheva, Tamar, and Shalhevet—I love you very much. Thank you for your understanding, love, laughter, and sharing in our mission to be a blessing to the world. You give me and Mommy much joy and *naches*. I wrote this book as a gift to you. I pray that you lead your lives filled with passion, purpose, Torah, joy, and a never-ending sense of wonder.

What is mine is yours. I can't adequately express my gratitude to my soul mate, best friend, and cheerleader, Diane. Your unconditional love, honesty, support, and belief in me constantly remind me of who I am and who I can become. You inspire me to realize my potential every day. You're a gift from God. I love you *Beahava Raba Leolam*.

God is everywhere. May we open our hearts and minds to his presence every moment of every day.

INTRODUCTION:
Creating a Life of Legacy:
How to Reverse Engineer Your Life

I'll never forget the call.

It was 1989 and, like most college students, I spent winter break in Florida looking for some sun. Stepping off the airplane and being greeted by a burst of warm air was the best. As I entered the terminal, I had the added benefit of being greeted by my maternal grandparents, who lived in North Miami Beach. Lounging at the pool, going on walks with them, or eating out, the experience was a wonderful way to decompress after an intense period of finals.

Although being the oldest of six children came with big brother responsibilities, life was great and my worries were minimal. That warm Wednesday afternoon in January, my grandparents and I spent the morning at the pool. We were just coming back when we received a call that would change my life forever: My mother had suffered a brain aneurysm. She was just forty-four years old.

We were in a daze. As we tried to comprehend the details, my father conveyed to us that my mother had felt a throbbing pain in her head and, in a whisper, asked him to call an ambulance. She was conscious when they carried her out of the house on a stretcher. In the seven minutes it took to speed through the streets, the only breath my father dared utter was a prayer to God to save his wife, my mother. But before she reached the emergency door, she fell into a coma. We all booked the next flight out of Florida to be with my mother. I couldn't believe what I'd heard. I prayed fervently as we rushed back home and sat vigil by her bedside. To this day, I remember being in the ICU with her, not knowing whether she was dead or alive. I thought I saw her move her eyelids. I held her hand, lingered with her touch, and gave her a kiss on her forehead. How could this be happening? Just yesterday we spoke, she laughed, and now, *within forty-eight hours*, she'd passed away, leaving her parents, a husband, and six children, ages eight to twenty-one, to mourn her loss.

My world—our world—was turned upside down in an instant. I didn't know how I could go on. My mother was my rock and source of strength. How could it be that she was no longer here?

I spoke at her funeral in front of hundreds of people in Atlanta, our hometown. She was buried in Israel, as is traditional in Judaism. I woke up in the middle of the night during shivah, the traditional Jewish period of mourning, as I couldn't sleep, and I frantically recorded stories that I remembered, and ones that people had shared, to ensure she wouldn't be forgotten. Although I returned to Yeshiva University after shivah for the spring semester, for days and months, I couldn't fathom the reality of my mom's sudden death. In the middle of class, I couldn't focus and I'd break down and cry. I took great comfort during the year in recording and reading my thoughts at the time of her death and the reflections of our family and friends.

Although the pain of my mother's absence will never disappear, I've realized that she is ever present in our lives in ways I never thought possible. Though she is not with me physically, I sense her presence, hear her voice, and feel her guidance and influence every day. There are moments when I may be searching for the right words to share in my role as a congregational rabbi, and if I listen carefully, she serves as a muse. I turn above and offer eternal thanks.

Over time, the call I'd received more than twenty-five years ago has evolved into a calling. Her passing instilled within me an acute awareness of the fragility of life and the gift of every day. I live with a heightened sense of urgency to realize my divine potential and to do my utmost every day to harness all of my energy and talents to help other people realize their potential as well.

In the past twenty years, I've come to appreciate that my personal awakening motivates me, defines me, and guides me to lead a life of meaning and impact. Through this experience, I discovered that I'm leading my life with greater passion and purpose. Rather than experiencing life in a casual way, I'm driven to maximize every moment.

When my mother died at forty-four, I knew she was young. Now that I'm in my forties myself, I think about my own mortality and am even more attuned to the stark reality that every second, every good-bye as someone leaves in the morning, and every milestone graduation or birthday could be the last.

In truth, almost everyone experiences such an awakening in their lives. There's a moment in all of our lives when we experience a wake-up call: a moment when the terra firma beneath the normal ebb and flow of life is shaken or stirred. You might call it an inner earthquake. For some it may, God forbid, be a death in the family or a personal illness. For others it may be an awakening due to the birth of a child or grandchild, or a wedding, a recent economic upheaval, the loss of a job, or challenges at work.

When we experience a brush with our own mortality, we ask ourselves, "How can I lead a more fulfilling and meaningful life?" As
Peter Lynch, the famed manager of Fidelity Magellan Fund, explained
upon his abrupt retirement in 1992, "There is more to life than money
and management."

We want more out of life. The most poignant expression of this
deep-seated desire emerges at a funeral when we are confronted with
our own mortality. For a brief time, we hear about the life of another
person—what they loved, who they touched, what they lived for, who
they influenced, and how they'll live on. As we leave the funeral, we
ask ourselves, "How will I be remembered?" We may be reminded
about the importance of family and pledge more time with our own
or reexamine our friendships or the infinite value of a good name.

But by the end of the day, if not sooner, the awakening dissipates or
becomes dormant, only to reemerge at another funeral or life-altering
event, when, once again, we ask ourselves whether we're maximizing
our potential and if we're truly happy and leading a life of impact. At
some point, every human being asks themselves these questions, but
all too often, the inspiration to act on them wafts away like a cloud
on a breezy summer day.

Whether rich or poor, black or white, believer or not, the innate
desire to lead a life of lasting influence resonates universally. Although
I'm an Orthodox rabbi, this book is for people of all faith traditions.
Regardless of your personal belief system, we all possess a deep-
rooted desire for a life of purpose.

I've had the privilege of sharing people's most intimate moments,
whether by a bedside in their final moments or guiding families
through death and the "after" life. The final words of a dying person
or a eulogy distill our core values into a clear and coherent mission for

life. How do we retain the feeling? How do we organize and orient our lives around our inner aspirations and actions every day? This book will help you unlock the secret. It will enrich your life, enhance your relationships, enable you to find inner joy and courage, and help you to pursue the life of your dreams.

The concept of reverse engineering your life stems from a belief in your capacity to unlock the divine spark within you. You're endowed with the gift of free choice, and every day and every encounter can be a transformative and eternal moment. How do we reverse engineer our lives? What if we could develop a strategy for living that would ensure a life of influence and impact while simultaneously motivating us to live in the moment?

We can understand the process by analyzing the mechanics of reverse engineering a product. In the conventional sense, reverse engineering is defined as the process of discovering the technological principles of a device, object, or system through analysis of its structure, function, and operation. It often involves taking something (e.g., a mechanical device, electronic component, or software program) apart and analyzing its workings in detail, or trying to make a new device or program that does the same thing without using or simply duplicating (without understanding) the original.

Imagine yourself as the CEO of a budding beverage company. On a trip to the Far East, you discover a "no calorie" drink that leaves you feeling like it's the best drink on Earth. You want to replicate the product and market it in the United States. You purchase a few cases and ship them back to your laboratory at corporate headquarters. You're ready to start your venture. The process of duplication contains three steps.

1. Analyze the ingredients of the beverage.
2. Develop a formula based on your findings.
3. Develop the new drink based on the recipe to produce a new, refreshing product.

What if we could reverse engineer our lives? What if we could develop principles for living that would ensure a life of influence and impact while simultaneously motivating us to live in the moment? That is the mission of this book. Having officiated at hundreds of funerals, sat at the bedside of the dying, and reflected on the value of a meaningful life, I've developed seven principles for reverse engineering your life.

In Chapter 1, "How Do You Want to Be Remembered?," you'll learn how to build a prototype of the life you aspire to lead. As in the process of scientific engineering, your model will be a 3-D one. Through a process of *discovery*, you'll be able to *design* a life to achieve your *destiny*. Once you envision the life of your dreams, in Chapters 2–8, we'll explore each of the seven principles in detail, be inspired by real-life stories, and gain hands-on tools to help you along the way.

In the past few years, I've shared the concept of applying reverse engineering to our personal lives with many people. The thirst for such a path is palpable. We live in a world that moves at lightning speed, and we know that we miss many moments and relationships that should be cherished. As a community, we're heartened when we witness acts of personal heroism and devotion to family, and we wish these exceptions were the norm.

The seven principles will provide a road map for you. Through the process of developing your best self by embracing these principles, you'll be able to start living the life now for which you want to be remembered after you're gone—your legacy. I challenge you to dig deep into your life. You're blessed with inherent gifts, and your life is trademarked. There is only one *you*. This book will enable you to discover the brand secret within you and motivate you to be your very best self. Not only will you experience more joy, meaning, and happiness, but you'll positively impact your friends and community in ways that will establish your personal legacy now and forever.

CHAPTER 1

How Do You Want to Be Remembered?

Alfred Nobel, the chemist who invented dynamite, had a unique experience that answered this question for him. When his brother Ludvig died, a French newspaper mistakenly wrote an obituary about Alfred entitled "The Merchant of Death." Shocked that he was viewed as the curator of death, Alfred did some soul-searching and decided to leave a different mark on the world by endowing the Nobel Prize with his wealth. He had the advantage of seeing his obituary in print before he had actually died. It was his wake-up call, and he chose to alter his life and legacy. He asked himself, "Is this the way I want to be remembered? Is this my legacy?" In that moment, he decided to take all of his wealth and create the Peace Prize. He said, "It's not only about the dynamite, but it's about making sure that I leave the world a better place." We rarely get that kind of preview, to hear another person's perception of us at the end of our lives.

In truth, such awakenings abound. How often do we leave a funeral or experience a sickness, a life transition, or a new job, and ask ourselves, "What will they say about me when I'm gone?" How many of you have felt that way when encountering an individual who's truly inspiring? You hear them speak and say to yourself, "Wait a second. Maybe I should be spending a little more time on what is truly important rather than on what is urgent." You're motivated. Then, about fifteen minutes later, you get a phone call or a text and get distracted, until the next moment of awakening happens.

We all experience moments when we gain clarity of mind and purpose and yearn to lead our lives a little bit fuller and better. It's precisely this brush with our own mortality that inspires us to lead lives of greater impact and import. But how long does that inspiration last?

In writing this book, I met with numerous celebrities for their insights. Their reflections are peppered throughout the book and notably in a section at the end of each chapter entitled "Celebrity Stirrings."

In my interview with film director, producer, actor, writer, and former child star Ron Howard, he reflected on the emotional trigger of a funeral for self-introspection.

> I've actually thought about that on the way back from funerals. I've actually had that specific reaction. I've also had the cautionary one where I'll leave a funeral, and I'll say, "He was a nice guy, but nobody really had much to say about him. What does that mean about the way he lived his life? He didn't do anything wrong, but he doesn't seem to have extended himself. He doesn't seem to have reached or ever gone the extra mile on behalf of an idea, or a person, or a principle." That's startling.

As a young guy, I didn't like funerals. I stayed away from them. As a kid I just avoided them. I didn't like my grandparents' funerals at all. My parents were very cool about it. Not formally very religious, but spiritual about the whole thing in a pretty healthy way. Somewhere along the line I began to appreciate them not only for the healing power that I could see visited upon the survivors, but I also realized that we need these summations. As a society, we need to take stock. It can be inspiring or, as I said, a little frightening.

The challenge is not simply to wish or dream that our lives will be different but to truly commit to making them so. How do we sustain the momentum that we gain from these awakening moments to truly achieve personal greatness?

Life isn't meant to be a highlight film. As a rabbi, I often get calls from people right before they're about to go to the hospital. They say, "Rabbi, pray for me. I believe in God. I want to come to services." Because they're experiencing some level of crisis, they're motivated to take stock of their lives and make changes. But once the crisis is resolved, they go back to who they were before, to life as usual.

Rabbi Menachem Mendel of Kotzk said, "My job in life is not to resurrect the dead; my job in life is to resurrect the living." How many times do you walk through life and wonder where the time went? Time can't be stopped, but it can be slowed down. How do we live life with that higher frequency, with that sense that every day is important?

Recently, I interviewed former mayor of New York Rudy Giuliani. I asked him, "Wouldn't it be really special if our country lived as if it was September 12 every day? Not September 11. Nobody wants to repeat what happened on September 11. However, on September

12, there was a greater sense in our country of our unifying values. We transcended our differences. We weren't focused on the partisan divide. We hugged our children a little bit tighter."

He replied, "Rabbi, I'm not sure how we'd get there, but I can tell you, I know what you mean. When I was the mayor of New York, I would oftentimes go into Shea Stadium with my Yankees cap on, and I would always be booed. There was one time when I knew things were different in the country. It was on the first game between the Yankees and the Mets that took place after September 11. I walked into Shea Stadium with my Yankees cap on and got a standing ovation. I knew the world was a little bit different."

I grew up in Atlanta. I was a Falcons fan, a Braves fan, a Hawks fan, and Flames fan of blessed memory. I didn't have any sports heroes on the bulletin board in my room. I had a poster over my bed with a phrase from the Jewish compilation Ethics of the Fathers: "If not now, when?" I grew up with a distinct sense that life has a purpose, that life is significant, that every moment can be something that we can harness for something great.

We've all experienced moments when we confront our mortality. These moments possess the potential for real change. Perhaps this explains a curious bit of wisdom from King Solomon, who wrote, "Better to go to a funeral than a wedding." How is that possible? We'd all rather be at a wedding. Here's the difference: The morning after a wedding, we might say, "It was fun. I had a good time. I ate too much," and so on. However, following a funeral, there's a chance that your life may be changed. You confront mortality and a life well lived, or tragically unrealized, and you may be stirred to reevaluate your own. The impact is resounding.

Developing a Prototype

The first step on your journey to reverse engineering your life is to develop a prototype. Reflect on how you want to be remembered. The question, "What will they say about you when you're gone?" is the trigger to awaken your inner dreams and aspirations.

This opening exercise is the foundation of your journey to spiritual greatness and a life of impact. If you don't have a goal in mind, you'll never achieve it. The temptation is to read the book without pausing for inner reflection. I'm sure this perusal would still be meaningful, but you can't optimize your potential without digging deep inside yourself. Who are you? Who do you want to be? How do you want to be remembered?

Take a quiet hour to answer these questions. If you only have a few minutes, start with one question to jumpstart the process of personal introspection. You may choose to watch a movie to get you in the mood. One of the most inspiring is *It's a Wonderful Life*. Psychologists have actually coined the phrase "the George Bailey Technique" as a strategy for contemplating the fragility and meaning of life. Think about what the world would be like without you. It will awaken you to the gifts that surround you.

> *"You've been given a great gift, George:*
> *a chance to see what the world*
> *would be like without you."*
>
> —Clarence Odbody, Angel Second Class

In the film, George Bailey constantly has his dreams thwarted because he always put his friends and family first. As a child, he wanted to travel to exotic locales and build big things like skyscrapers and airstrips. However, due to different crises (his father's sudden death, threats of his father's Building and Loan business being dissolved unless George took over, and the stock market crash, to name a few), he always put his dreams on the back burner so he could take care of other people.

One Christmas Eve, George's absentminded uncle, Billy, misplaces $8,000 of the Building and Loan's funds. Losing the money would mean bankruptcy for the Bailey Building and Loan and criminal charges for George. In desperation, George decides to commit suicide so his family can cash in his $15,000 life insurance policy and pay off the $8,000 debt.

Just before George leaps from a bridge to his icy, watery death, his guardian angel, Clarence Odbody (a second-class angel who has yet to earn his wings), jumps into the river and pretends he's drowning. George, being the bighearted guy that he is, saves Clarence. While they're drying off, Clarence tries to talk George out of killing himself. When George bitterly wishes that he'd never been born, through angelic powers, Clarence is able to show him what his family and Bedford Falls would've been like had he never existed.

It becomes a hellhole.

George's younger brother, Harry, dies when he falls through the ice in a skating accident because George wasn't there to save him; his mother is a bitter widow; and quaint Bedford Falls is Pottersville, a sleazy town, because people are living in slum apartments instead of the nice homes George's Building and Loan funded. Worst of all, George's wife is an old maid, and none of their four beautiful children exist.

As you can guess, George sees the light and begs God to live again.

His wish granted, he runs joyously through the streets yelling "Merry Christmas!" to everybody. He arrives home to find the authorities with a warrant in hand for his arrest, but George doesn't care. He's so happy to hold and kiss his kids. His wife comes in shortly after, followed by what seems like the entire town. The townsfolk all donate enough money to save George and the Building and Loan, George's old childhood friend Sam Wainwright wires him $25,000 from overseas, and George's war hero brother, Harry, arrives to declare George "the richest man in Bedford Falls." Among the giant pile of cash, George finds a copy of *Tom Sawyer* from Clarence that had this inscription: "Dear George: Remember, no man is a failure who has friends. P.S. Thanks for the wings! Love, Clarence." It's at this moment that George realizes what a wonderful life he really has. By seeing what the world would be like without him, he comes to a greater understanding and appreciation for the true richness of his blessings.

Now it's your turn to start the process of leading the life you want to lead and be remembered for. This is your wake-up call, your moment of truth. Pick one person, place, or event in your life that brings you happiness and satisfaction, and write down in a journal the various ways it might not have happened. Then imagine your life without that person/place/event and write that down, too. The more frequently you do this exercise, the more grateful, optimistic, and hopeful you'll be.

Let's go deeper and confront an even tougher question.

> *"The greatest treasure that a human being possesses is the power of speech, because through this, he is greater than all other creatures."*
>
> —Rabbi Aharon Halevi of Barcelona

In his memoirs, Rabbi Emanuel Feldman, formerly a prominent rabbi in Atlanta, wrote about the most difficult question he was asked in his entire rabbinic career. He once received a call from a woman who was desperate to meet with him. When they met, he asked her what was so urgent and how he could help. The woman said, "Rabbi, I have cancer of the larynx and next week I'm having surgery to have my larynx removed" (this was before the invention of the voice box, a device that emits an electric voice when placed next to the larynx). She asked him, "Rabbi, I'll never be able to speak again, but I can choose the final words my lips will ever utter. What should they be?" Rabbi Feldman described this as the most difficult question he had ever been asked. He encouraged her to recite a prayer and told her, "You can pray in any language and God's door is always open." They recited a prayer together, and as he left she remarked, "Tonight, I'll say another prayer but you pray for me too. Thank you for visiting. I'm still frightened but a lot less than before."

What would you answer and what would you choose? Would your last words be an expression of love to a spouse or child, a statement of your faith, a prayer that you offer, or a song that you sing? If you could only speak one more time, what would you say? And if that's what you'd say if you only had one last chance to speak, why not say it now? Why not value every opportunity to communicate as if it is your last?

What do you stand for? What is truly important in your life, and how do you want to be remembered? Leave your facade behind. Don't wait until, God forbid, you or someone you love makes you question all that you thought was secure in life. Don't wait for the emotional earthquake to get serious about life. By then, it will be too late. Start the process now. You want meaning and joy in your life. Dig deep and discover who you are and who you want to be.

Below are questions for personal reflection.

Developing a Life of Legacy Prototype:
A Personal Meditation

How do you want to be remembered?

1. By your family
2. By your community
3. By the world

_____

_____

_____

_____

_____

Writing Your Own Eulogy

If you had to write your own eulogy, what would it say? Use the following questions as inspiration, and then craft a eulogy for your own funeral.

1. What would you do if you had twenty-four hours to live? Why?

_____

_____

_____

_____

_____

2. What is worth fighting for?

_____

_____

_____

_____

3. In your life so far, what have you taken a risk for or gone out of your comfort zone for?

_____

_____

_____

_____

4. You have five words to write on your headstone. What are they?

_____

_____

_____

_____

5. When you're feeling low, what song do you play to lift your mood and inspire you? Why?

_____

_____

_____

_____

6. Is there a phrase that you find yourself saying frequently when you're under stress? When you're happy or grateful?

_____

_____

_____

7. Describe your best day or your best self.

_____

_____

_____

_____

8. What is your favorite Bible verse, poem, or motto?

_____

_____

_____

_____

9. Why are you here? What is your life mission? What do you hope to achieve?

_____

_____

_____

_____

10. What are your dreams? How can you realize them?

_____

_____

_____

_____

I've conducted Reverse Engineer Your Life seminars across the country, and developing a prototype of the person you are and who you'd like to be is one of the most critical steps in establishing your ideal vision of yourself to aspire to every day. I'm always struck by the heartfelt responses of many people. Everyone deep down wants a more inspired and authentic life. Rarely do we find the sacred space to listen to our inner voice and solidify our most cherished values. Take a moment to read some of the responses from the seminars:

- I'm Larry from Chicago. I'd like them to say that I was a mensch (a person of integrity and honor), loving, caring, resourceful, and knowledgeable.
- I'm Belle from Manila, Philippines. Five words on my tombstone: How great is our God. What described my life: Love of God and love of others. The third is twenty-four hours to live, what to do and why: All that I still can do for God.
- My five words: An ordinary guy extraordinarily blessed.
- I'm Lacy and I went with hashtags for my five words: #goofy, #sweet, #giving, #foodie, #ultimate napper. On my tombstone: Go in the direction of your dreams. Live the life you've always imagined.
- I'm Wayne from Alpena, Michigan. I only did five words. That's as far as I could get: Funeral Director: Laughed, loved, served.
- I'm Keith and my five words: Best day of my life. On my tombstone: It's all good. I'm the fifteenth of seventeen children. My mom and dad were married for fifty-eight years. I'm tremendously blessed. I've had the privilege of never tasting alcohol, never smoking any cigarettes, never doing a drug. I live in the best country in the world.
- I'm Frank from Philadelphia: Loved God and family and satisfied with my life. On the five words: True to himself and convictions. For the twenty-four hours, I felt that I've known God. I've tried to live my life, and I'm not afraid to die, so I'd continue to do what I'd normally be doing in that twenty-four-hour period.
- I'm Tim from Michigan. Five words on my tombstone: Husband, father, son, brother. The inscription: He gave up himself to others. If

I had twenty-four hours to live, what would I do and why? Tell people they mattered to me. They made an impact on my life.

- I'm Mark from Flemington, New Jersey. My five words on the tombstone: Told you I was sick. One from U2 would be my song of choice. I would spend the last twenty-four hours talking to my family and friends to reassure them that I was a much better person for all they did for me.

- I'm Tim from Arizona. My five words would be: Always remember families are forever. On the backside of my headstone, it would read: May angels sing thee to thy rest.

- I'm Ejay from Covington, Louisiana. My five words would be: He did better than he deserved. My life verse has always been Proverbs 3:5–6: "Trust in the Lord with all your heart, and lean not on your own understanding but in all your ways acknowledge Him, and He will direct your path." I'd say to my family, "This has just been a soldier in here, and my time is up."

- I'm Ruth from Clinton, New Jersey. My five words are: There's power in a hug. My sentence would be: A woman of care, respect, and honor. In my last twenty-four hours, I'd cross the country and hug my son, and tell him he's capable of doing absolutely anything.

✺

"I expect to pass through this world but once.
Any good therefore that I can do, or any kindness or
abilities that I can show to any fellow creature,
let me do it now. Let me not defer it or neglect it,
for I shall not pass this way again."

—*William Penn*

CHAPTER 2

Principle No. 1:
Discover Your Elijah Moment

Y ou were born with a purpose. You're not an accident or a random combination of cells. As you read this book, contemplate that it is not by chance that you're reading this chapter. There's a message for you to glean for personal growth that was intended just for you today.

What is life's purpose? Why are you here? Why were you created in this time and place in history? Regardless of your faith tradition or lack thereof, we all believe deep down that we were created with a purpose, and we yearn to make a difference in the world. We hope to leave the world a better place.

In the world of mysticism, every soul descends into a body with a divine mission: to emulate the Almighty. God created the world with love, and each of us serves as his partner to spread his light and be a blessing.

It's no wonder that Judaism teaches that we have an obligation to greet every human being with a smile on our face. No encounter is random. If I meet someone or pass by someone and our faces meet, a possibility emerges for a soul connection and a moment of eternal impact. I call these encounters "Elijah moments."

Who is Elijah? He was a prophet appointed by God who appeared periodically throughout history to shepherd the Jewish people. You may have heard stories about an Elijah appearance. I want to share mine with you. I spotted him at the Stamford Cove on Long Island Sound and he lives in Springdale, Connecticut. He gave me a push just when I needed it most.

For the past numbers of years, our synagogue has conducted a sunrise service at the cove prior to the high holidays. Every year I wonder whether it's worth doing (particularly at 5:00 a.m.) because the crowds are so small. This past year, the prayers were beautiful and uplifting as always. One of our members remarked at the end how much he looked forward to the experience every year. What happened next was hard to believe. As we arrived at the parking lot to get into our cars, a man in his fifties, wearing shorts and a shirt, greeted us. He exclaimed to us, "My mishpacha, my family, Shanah Tovah! Happy New Year!" He had no idea I was a rabbi.

I asked him if he had a place to go for Rosh Hashanah and he responded, "I knew you were going to ask me that. I don't have a place but I have little money for membership. Are you going to treat me like Elijah and open the door for me?" I responded, "Of course, you are welcome."

He then reminisced about how the last time he felt a Jewish connection was in the 1980s when he was welcomed into a Mitzvah tank (a vehicle used as an educational and "outreach center," like a mobile mini-synagogue) in New York City and donned the ritual phylacteries (the small black leather boxes containing parchments from Scripture). He shared, "I'll never forget that the fellows told me I looked so authentic!"

Then he said something I'll never forget: "Every year I always look for you guys on the Sunday before Rosh Hashanah and wonder whether you'll need me for the ten people required for the prayer service. This year, I felt a bit embarrassed since I was walking around in shorts, but as you were leaving, I thought I'd approach you and introduce myself with the word mishpacha [family]."

I couldn't believe it. Here was a man who was looking for me and believing in me when I needed it most. He invoked the prophet Elijah to alert me and us that Elijah may be in our midst—all we have to do is open the door. In the years since that first encounter, we see him every year, and he joins our service.

Throughout history, Elijah has appeared in the most mysterious places. In one story, a student of the Baal Shem Tov (a mystic who is considered to be the founder of Hasidic Judaism) felt that after much preparation, he was deserving of a vision of the prophet Elijah. His master instructed him to visit a certain town and ask to be hosted at the home of a specific family. "Make sure to bring them food," the Baal Shem Tov added. The student eagerly packed a wagon full of food and set off. Upon arriving, he was directed to an old, dilapidated house, the home of a poor widow with many young children. The student spent Shabbat (the Jewish Sabbath) with them and was only too happy to share his mountain of food. But Elijah never showed up.

The Baal Shem Tov then instructed the student to try again the next week. As he approached the door, he heard a child's plaintive voice say, "But what will we eat on Shabbat?" A reassuring voice replied, "Don't worry. Just like Elijah came last week, he'll come this week again!"

What does it mean to be an Elijah? The student set out to find Elijah in some remote location only to realize that Elijah lay within. It was in that moment of recognition when he realized that he was the one the family was waiting for and that he was the agent of kindness. He knew that his life embodied a mission beyond himself.

What if we were to discover our Elijah moments every day? I believe that not only would we lead more impactful lives but the world would be a radically different place. When I walk into a coffee shop, my office, or my home, I ask myself what I can do in the next few minutes to make someone's day. It's a vastly different way of looking at the world and one that will transform you and your surroundings.

Discovering your Elijah moment will alter your perception of every encounter. Your day will not be simply about moving from one event to another but about harnessing the latent potential in every encounter to connect one soul to the next and make a difference.

In this chapter, you'll learn how to become an Elijah in the following ways:

1. By discovering the difference in a minute.
2. By anticipating opportunities for impact.
3. By renewing appreciation of your daily mission.
4. By increasing happiness and inner joy.
5. By becoming a ripple that creates a tidal wave.

What are you waiting for? Let the journey begin.

Foundations

What does it mean to discover your Elijah moment? The concept emerges from the "standing room only" phenomenon at a funeral. We've all experienced it before. You go to the funeral of a loved one and notice that there's a person there whom you don't recognize. If you could ask the deceased who the person was, he or she wouldn't know either. If you ask the family, they don't know either. Yet the person stands on the side to honor the deceased because of one moment in time when he or she made a difference in their life. Perhaps it was a fleeting encounter, when one human touched another and made an indelible impact.

The roots of the Elijah moment emerge from the encounter of Moses at the burning bush. God appeared to him as described in the Bible and charged him with the mission of liberating the Jewish people from Egypt. We're all familiar with the story, if not from the Bible then from the movie *The Ten Commandments*. Amazingly, Moses initially refused to go. He argued with God and claimed that he was not capable of speaking to Pharaoh on the Almighty's behalf for, after all, he stuttered. How would Pharaoh understand him?

God responded to Moses in anger. He replied, "Who do you think gave you the power to see? Who gave you the power to speak? It is I. If I am offering you the opportunity to serve as an ambassador for me, know that I believe in you!" This captures the essence of the Elijah moment. If we're placed in a situation of potential impact, it must be because of the innate possibility of realizing the holiness of the moment.

I'd venture to say that we've all experienced these moments. It's the joy we feel deep down when we sense our actions are fully aligned with a higher purpose. It's a moment when our hearts are full. It could be as simple as giving a stranded motorist a ride into town or providing change for the customer ahead of you who came up short when he was paying for his groceries. Or it could be of greater import, such as witnessing a grandchild being born. In that moment, all seems right. As described by a grandmother whose daughter gave birth to a girl, "As I sat silently with my daughter and her daughter, I sensed the presence of my mother and grandmother as well." We feel entwined with the cords of generational continuity. Grandchildren are the dividends of investment, when we can say we have passed the baton to the next generation. That is an Elijah moment.

One of the clearest examples of this phenomenon for me occurred while visiting Denver. I was privileged to name a baby for a couple whose wedding I had presided over a few years ago. The moment was bittersweet, as the baby was named after her great-grandfather, who was now deceased. Yet when sharing blessings among the family members following the service, when asked for her thoughts, the only words the great-grandmother could share were "My heart is full," for she knew that although her husband was not physically present, the birth of this baby embodied her and her husband's highest aspirations.

I'll always be grateful to an Elijah who ignited my mother's spirit in me. Although she is not physically present, I feel her presence daily. Some days the sense is more acute than others. I had one such moment when I found a sealed letter on my desk addressed to me from Gary Lavitt, a family friend for close to fifty years. I opened the envelope and read the following: "Dear Dani, In going through my possessions in preparation for moving to Israel, I came across the enclosed. Note the postmark date. I thought you would enjoy having this thank-you note—from you to me—handwritten by your mother. All the best, Gary."

The postmark on the envelope was October 19, 1967, a little more than six weeks after I was born. The card was embossed with the words "Sandra and Herbert" and contained a note in my mother's distinctive handwriting. With two Hebrew letters in the upper right-hand corner (Bet and Heh, signifying the help of God), she wrote, "Dear Gary, thank you very much for the lovely outfit. I am really looking forward to wearing my first pair of long pants. [She had underlined the word "long."] Daniel Yaakov Cohen."

When I read the note the first time, I began to cry. I've now worn long pants for more than four decades! But in all seriousness, my mother's letter, which had come to me twenty-five years after she was gone, awakened within me the unconditional love of my mom for me, a parent for a child.

As we grow older and more independent, we tend to overlook all of the sleepless nights, time, love, and devotion our parents showered on us, as well as the joy in our births and the hopes and dreams they had for us. If we're fortunate to still have living parents, we need to let them know how much we love them. If our parents have died, we need to remember that we are their living legacy.

I'm eternally grateful to Gary, an Elijah, for spending a few minutes and the cost of a stamp to give me a priceless, cherished reminder of my mother. In his decision to write me, he had enlivened her spirit and made it a bit brighter. We don't write letters as often as we did before such free access to technology, but sometimes letters are worth saving forever. Perhaps you know someone who has lost a parent with whom you were close. Take a few minutes to be an Elijah and send them a note or call them. We can be a bridge from Heaven to Earth.

Are you making a difference in the world? What will people say about you? I'd venture that most if not all of us can answer in the affirmative. We can identify a person who we've impacted in a meaningful way. Perhaps it was a child, a friend, or a coworker to whom we offered support, wisdom, or a helping hand.

I'd like to share two brief stories to illustrate more Elijah moments. Both occurred to friends, one on the West Side of New York City and the other in a parking lot in West Hartford, Connecticut. When walking down the street in the midst of a mass of people in Manhattan, faces become blurred. One person blends into the next as we navigate the sidewalks. It's a human obstacle course, and people become objects to ignore. Yet we all know that every human being has a story and a soul. Every person is created with holiness and purpose. All it takes is one meeting face-to-face, one gesture of kindness, one encounter, to transform the anonymity into a heartfelt moment. Recently, a young man shared the following story with me:

My wife Elisa and I were walking down Columbus Avenue one afternoon. We passed a homeless man who asked if we would buy him lunch. I immediately agreed to buy him lunch and asked him what his preference was. He asked if I would buy him a slice of pizza, and as it happened, there was a place right near us. As I was walking to the restaurant, he shouted out to me if I wouldn't mind getting him a slice with extra cheese. I turned and we started to laugh at each other. I then asked if he wanted pepperoni or anything else, and he said, "No, just extra cheese." While I was getting the food, my wife was engaging him in conversation. When I returned with his lunch, he and I started to talk. I then realized just how important it was to engage another person in conversation to make him or her feel as much a part of humanity as myself, no matter what an individual's circumstance may be.

It was an Elijah moment in the heart of one the busiest cities in the world, amid millions of people, finding meaning in one moment.

Another friend of mine discovered her Elijah moment in a parking lot in West Hartford. I led a discussion on the topic of living inspired. I began with a request: Share a peak moment when you felt connected to God. One woman shared the following: "A few weeks ago, I was getting out of my car at the Big Y parking lot. Out of the corner of my eye, I saw an elderly man with orthopedic shoes slowly exiting his car and noticed that one of his shoes was untied. I'm not sure what possessed me, but I went over to him and asked if I could help him tie his shoes, as I knew it would be hard for him to bend down."

With tears in her eyes, she shared that in that instant, she felt closer to God than almost ever before in her life. Almost the entire group welled up in tears. She wondered why she became so emotional when sharing her story. I explained that in those few seconds when she intuitively sensed her ability to become a messenger for God, her soul was on fire. It was her Elijah moment.

Life is intended to be lived this way.

The Slonimer Rebbe, a Hasidic master, shares a stirring idea based on the teaching of the holy mystic Rabbi Isaac Luria. At the end of our lives, how will we be judged by God? Rabbi Luria explains that the most haunting question will be: Did we realize our mission in this world? It's a question that speaks to the heart of our personal potential to serve as angels on Earth.

Most important, the mystics suggest that not only do we have a mission in life but one that changes from one day to the next. Just as God renews creation every day, he also renews our responsibility to the world. Every day, we encounter new people, new circumstances, and new opportunities, and we are called upon, with the God-given talents we possess, to rise to the occasion—every day. There's no room for complacency. This is the bar. It's very high. What did each of us do today to uplift another soul? What can we do today to be an Elijah? It could be in a coffee shop in Manhattan or in a supermarket parking lot. It could be as simple as a call to offer support to a coworker, friend, or family member. Each of us can be an Elijah.

> *"How wonderful it is that nobody*
> *need wait a single moment before starting*
> *to improve the world."*
>
> —Anne Frank

When do we remember a face? When is a person not forgotten? What memories will linger and endure forever? The Torah teaches us that God remembers an act of kindness for thousands of generations. Think for a moment about an experience in your life when someone extended themselves to you, offered a hello or a helping hand, and made all the difference in that one moment. I'm sure a few examples come to mind. Coming to a new school, place of work, or organization is never easy. Transitions are hard. It's possible to be in a room with hundreds of people and still feel lonely. Yet one hello can wash away that feeling, warm our hearts, and clear a path for connection.

When I arrived at Yeshiva University during orientation week as a freshman, I was overwhelmed by the course offerings and new environment. Coming from a small Jewish high school in Atlanta with my father as principal and my mom as a teacher, and a class size of fifteen, New York City and the college stirred excitement and trepidation within me. What classes would I choose? What would my major be? Who would my friends be? To this day I'll never forget the kindness of a senior, Ronnie Rosenberg. On the first day of orientation, he introduced himself and sat down with me to help me organize my schedule and show me the "lay of the land." He introduced me to some of his peers and instilled within me the confidence to forge ahead. His smile, wisdom, and generosity of spirit transformed my experience and laid the groundwork for my experience at YU.

Think about it for a moment. Ronnie made a conscious decision to reach out to me, to move outside his comfort zone. It didn't cost him any money, only his knowledge, time, and a smile. That exchange and his kindness still live in me more than twenty-five years later.

What will you do today that will be worthy of future memory? What will you do today to be the Elijah the world is waiting for?

When confronted with the question of whether we've realized our full potential for making an impact on people and the world around us, we realize we fall short. Count the people you meet in a given day, the e-mails you receive, or the requests for advice. There are dozens of encounters. Is it not possible that we could've done more, given more, or listened more to such people? Of course! The question is not meant to depress you but to alert you to the numerous possibilities we possess for impact. The nature of life is that we contemplate the opportunities missed and lament what we could've done for another person if given a second chance.

To go a step further, think about the people who didn't ask for help who we could've reached out to touch. Think about the people we pass by in the store or in line at the local coffee shop. Did we greet them with a warm smile and wish them a great day? Did we exchange a warm glance with a cashier or simply keep our eyes on our personal devices? Imagine if you looked up and smiled at someone. Perhaps the person was having a tough day and by acknowledging them, you've made an impact on their lives. Did you know that there are angels in the subway? In the rush of a train passing through the underground, one human being in the briefest of encounters can change a person's life.

We rarely know a person's backstory. One of my favorite people is a guy named Sydney who I see every morning at our local Starbucks. Like me, he's on a mission from God (sounds a bit like the Blues Brothers). We met from simply spending time together in the early morning hours. He sips his tea as he meditates and reads the Bible and I drink my coffee and prepare mentally for the day.

Sydney is an executive in Stamford but also serves as a deacon in his church. Most important in his life is his mission to offer support to people in need. Like me, he finds the hustle and bustle of a coffee shop, and many of the same people coming in and out each day, an opportunity to befriend someone and offer much-needed encouragement and counsel. I often say I see more people on a weekday in Starbucks than in the synagogue.

I shared the Elijah moment principle with Sydney and he shared his story with me. An angel on the subway in New York City changed his life and motivated him to be an Elijah to others.

Back in 1996, I experienced tremendous difficulty in my personal life and as a result became very discouraged and depressed. I found it very difficult to get through life on a daily basis and spent a lot of time with my parents to get the needed moral support.

One evening while coming home from work, I met an elderly gentleman on the NYC No. 5 train heading uptown from Wall Street. He came on the train at Fourteenth Street and immediately saw the sadness in my eyes. He reached out to me and started a conversation, questioning how I was feeling. I was so desperate that I came off the next stop at Forty-Second Street and bared my soul to a complete stranger. He was a kind and compassionate listener. After pouring my soul out to him for an hour, he assured me that things would get better, and he gave me his phone number to call him whenever I needed a listening ear.

I called him for five consecutive days and spoke about the many things that were on my mind. He just listened. By day number six, I had a very supernatural experience. I felt my heavy burdens physically lifting off my body, and felt a strong sense of God entering in.

Ever since that event, I started a ministry for reaching out to strangers. A stranger reached out to me and made the difference that I needed. I was then led by God to encourage others during the very early morning hours at a Starbucks location. My soul now sings at Starbucks every morning. There are times when I think he was an angel.

One anonymous man on a subway saw the pain in Sydney's eyes. He offered a listening ear and encouragement. It was one moment in time on a train that transported thousands of passengers every day. The man sensed an opportunity to reach out and make a difference in Sydney's life. We'll never know what motivated him. In the end, maybe he listened to Sydney for a sum total of a few hours over the course of six days. But in that short amount of time, Sydney's life was transformed forever. Wow! Who will you be an Elijah for today?

> *"Nothing can make our lives, or*
> *the lives of other people, more beautiful*
> *than perpetual kindness."*

—Leo Tolstoy

Our deepest joy emerges when we know we've touched another human being. Our souls soar when we sense we make a difference in the world. Reverse engineering our lives is about maximizing our divine potential every day. It's about not wasting a second and developing a mind-set for maximizing every moment. It's about embodying the philosophy of life rooted in the biblical idea that we're all in this world for a reason. When we wake up in the morning, it's for a purpose. The goal of the day is not just getting through it but unlocking the sparks within it and making them holy.

> *"True happiness . . .*
> *is not attained through self-gratification,*
> *but through fidelity to a*
> *worthy purpose."*
>
> —Helen Keller

How do we lead a life of infinite impact? How do we lead the lives now for how we want to be remembered when we're gone?

The most important strategy is discovering your Elijah moment. It's realizing that one person cannot change the world, but we can change the world of one person every day. It's about living with a heightened awareness that each day offers a new opportunity to shine.

Rabbi Adin Steinsaltz, a spiritual mentor, teacher, social critic, and philosopher, who *Time* magazine referred to as a "once-in-a-millennium scholar," said, "Every soul is a fragment of the divine light. As a spark, a part containing something of the whole, the soul's essential wholeness cannot be achieved except through effort, through work with the greater whole." The more we invest outside ourselves, the more eternal we'll be.

Jewish tradition distinguishes between Chaye Sha'ah (temporal life) and Chaye Olam (eternal life)—what is urgent and what is important. Urgent matters pass within the hour but important matters last for eternity. It's urgent that a businessperson be clever, but it's important that he or she be wise. It's urgent that our children get good grades, but it's important that they are good people.

Across the faith traditions, gathering for meals offers a time for families to bond, taste the traditions, and smell the hearth of the holiday. We can all look back on a comfort food in our homes that made the time even more memorable. Without the warm aroma and tasty bread, the experience would not be the same.

I'd like to share a story with you about a man whose legacy lives on due to the care he exhibited to ensure that every home had bread for the holiday. In the Jewish faith, holiday bread is known as challah, and it's eaten at the Sabbath meal every Friday night and Saturday lunch. Bakeries on Friday mornings are bustling with people purchasing fresh-baked challah for the Sabbath.

Elliot Waldstreicher owned the Harbor Bake Shop and was always insistent that his bakery would never run out of challahs on Friday afternoons. If they ran out, he would tell his staff that even if it meant baking an entire batch of challahs for just two people, he never wanted anyone to go home without a challah. Can we imagine the thousands of challahs that enhanced Friday night dinners and Saturday lunches? Despite the hectic place of a successful bake shop on Fridays, he made sure that every Jew who wanted a challah did not leave empty-handed because, for that Jew, that challah made all the difference.

I was awakened to the capacity of each of us to seize Chaye Olam—eternal life—when I had the blessing of being with Elliot just moments before he died. After we recited the Psalms and prayers with him, I reminded him of a conversation from a few days before that we had had with his family, where we'd talked about the fact that even after the soul departs the body, it lives on and derives pleasure in knowing that the time in this world forged an eternal impact. Moments before his soul departed from his body, I sensed he was at peace in knowing that he did his best in his time in this world by not living for the hour but in living for eternity.

In my mind, Elliot was a man who built for eternity. Not only did he raise wonderful children, grandchildren, and great grandchildren (may they be blessed), but, thank God, he also knew the importance of a loaf of challah bread. As Elliot lived, so must we.

We must live every day as if we believe in the world to come. Every moment and every encounter can affect eternity. When I was speaking with my dad one day, he told me that he was awakened to this reality by one of his close friends, Geoff Frisch, who passed away a few years ago at the age of sixty-five. Geoff was a businessman who became engaged with Jewish life and learning later in life and served as the president of Yeshiva High School in Atlanta, where my father had served as principal.

My dad shared that when Geoff was in sales, he would always say, "I'm not concerned whether someone buys from me or not but whether we connected as two human beings. If I can make someone smile or make a difference in someone's life, then regardless of the material benefit, I know that I'm living for eternity."

Being an Elijah means living life every day with an awareness of our capacity to be the Almighty's agents on Earth. It's one thing to sense this mission at life-cycle events and another to be conscious of our role all the time.

God calls on us to examine our mission awareness because he cares about us and believes in us. He knows that each of us can be an Elijah, an agent for fixing the world and elevating it. The more we lead our lives in sync with our mission, the more satisfying our lives will be. When we embrace our particular calling, we will live inspired! Mark Twain expressed this idea succinctly when he wrote, "The two most important days of our lives are the day we are born and the day we understand why."

On a personal level, I grew up with this awareness. As I mentioned earlier, the decor of my bedroom was not a picture of a superhero or a sports star but a saying from the Ethics of the Fathers: "If not now, when?" In subtle ways, my parents tried to instill within me the value of every moment and a sense of purpose. Unfortunately, we don't always live with this sense of urgency and possibility. Because my mother died suddenly at the young age of forty-four, to this day I live with a stronger sense of the fragility of life, and even more with an innate passion to infuse every moment with infinite holiness.

An Elijah moment signifies that you know you're in the right place at the right time. We began this chapter by reflecting on the foundation of the Elijah moment principle. We're all on Earth for a transcendent purpose. Every hour offers an opportunity for meaning and impact. God will sometimes orchestrate the moment for us and we only need to rise to the occasion.

The following two stories reflect how a higher power guides our lives and enables us to realize our divine potential and purpose.

Twenty-five years ago my mother was diagnosed with lung cancer and was given three months to live. We were extremely close and shared the same sense of humor. As a busy twenty-eight-year-old funeral director and just finishing work at 10:00 p.m. on the Fourth of July, I was heading home to my wife and newborn daughter. I told my wife that I felt I needed to stop by and see my mom before coming home.

When I arrived, my mom was waiting for me with a big smile and said, "Come sit with me on the couch and we can watch the Boston Pops play to the fireworks show." Being ill, my five-feet-three robust mom was now smaller and a bit frail. I am six-feet-five and almost 300 lbs. She said, "Lie back and relax on the couch with me," and I said, "Ma, I'm going to crush you." She asked again, and when I leaned back and crushed her, we both started to laugh so hard that we cried! I laid back again gently, and she cradled me like a baby. Right then the "Battle Hymn of the Republic" came on (her favorite song: "Glory, glory, hallelujah!"), and she said, "You have to promise me to play this at my funeral and tell everyone to remember me with smiles and not tears." I promised her, and one week later on July 11, my mom was remembered with smiles (and some tears). That was my Elijah moment.

I am a NODA (No One Dies Alone) volunteer at Stamford Hospital. We stay with patients who are at the end of their lives who don't have loved ones available to be with them. We become their loved ones as they leave this world. In September I sat with a cognitively disabled man several times. At my first visit, he was awake and I fed him vanilla ice cream. By my last visit, he was heavily sedated and nearing the end of his life. I held his hand and somehow felt even more connected to this patient than I had to others I had sat with. A few weeks ago I shared my experience with my family and found out that this gentle man's father was the doctor who delivered me in Stamford Hospital in 1956. His father was there to help my arrival into this world and I was there to help his son's departure fifty-eight years later. That was my Elijah moment!

Be an Elijah. Never underestimate our potential through our actions to transform any moment into an eternal one.

Strategies

Living in the Moment

In the song "If Not Now," Tracy Chapman sings, "We all must live our lives, always feeling, always thinking, the moment has arrived." We never know when the moment might be, but we must always be ready and anticipate opportunities. They're everywhere! A couple of years ago, a close friend of mine, Pastor Greg Doll, partnered with me in creating the Elijah Moment Campaign. In a world with increasing acts of violence, we encouraged people to flood the world with acts of kindness. We asked people to share their deliberate acts of kindness and to inspire others to do the same. We launched a Facebook page to share ideas and inspire deliberate acts of kindness. Connecticut Senator Richard Blumenthal even made a statement on the US Senate floor about the Elijah Moment Campaign. The opportunities for Elijah moments are endless. One of the secrets to discovering your Elijah moment is reflected in the words of Henry James, who wrote, "Try to be one of those on whom nothing is lost."

Looking back on our lives, we can probably identify seemingly insignificant moments when we made a courageous decision. At the time it may have seemed trivial, but in retrospect it made all the difference in the world. With practice and in reflection, you'll learn to recognize the potential magnitude of every moment. You'll gain the ability and the aptitude to live your life with courage.

When we live consciously and thoughtfully, we enrich and elevate the world. How often do we look back on the day and wonder where the time has gone? How often are we so immersed in our personal technological device that we miss the opportunity to have a human encounter?

I'll never forget my Elijah moment when listening to the radio one morning in my car. The words could've gone in one ear and out the other, but I'm grateful I tuned in to a higher frequency that day. On the morning of September 11, I picked up a coffee at Starbucks. As I got into my car, I heard a brief comment on the radio from an NYC police officer. He was touched when a woman gave him twenty dollars and thanked him for his service to the city. The impetus came during the anniversary of 9/11—a moment in time when our nation united and expressed deep appreciation to all those in uniform who serve and protect us.

In that instant, I debated in my mind between eternal life and temporal life. I was thinking about building eternity at 8:30 that Tuesday morning. Little did I know that God was clearly serving as my copilot. I suddenly felt the urge to park my car and go back to Starbucks. I'd always heard about the power of random acts of kindness, and I'd tried practicing them a few times, but it seemed that today would be a good day to do so in commemoration of 9/11.

I went back into the store and handed the cashier a few dollars and asked her to pay for the next person in line as a reminder of the spirit of kindness and unity that emerged after 9/11.

The recipient of my gift was grateful and surprised. He told me that he was a retired NYC police officer who'd been at Ground Zero on 9/11. He'd gotten home from an overnight shift at 8:00 a.m., and when the planes hit the towers, he was called back down. We reminisced about the moment, but we both expressed the hope that we could not only commemorate the day but harness the memory of it to foster a greater sense of appreciation for all who serve our communities and nation.

I got back into my car, listened to the moment of silence at 8:46, and knew that no act of kindness enters a void. One gift to a police officer in NYC broadcast on CBS 880 was heard in Stamford and spurred an act of kindness to a retired NYPD officer in Stamford, Connecticut. In fifteen minutes, God had guided me in living for eternity.

Tool Box

❶ **Smile power:** Wherever and whenever, share a smile. Make someone feel great!

❷ **Pay it forward at your local coffee shop.** It's contagious.

❸ **Give thanks every day to one important person in your life.** Make a list of people for whom you are grateful for even the smallest acts of kindness, then thank them. Renew the list every week.

The Ripple Effect

*"Everything we do, even the slightest thing
we do, can have a ripple effect and repercussions
that emanate. If you throw a pebble into the
water on one side of the ocean, it can create
a tidal wave on the other side."*

—Victor Webster

During our Elijah Moment Campaign, we launched flash mobs of kindness. We asked five people to descend on a local shop and asked them to "pay it forward" and offer a cup of coffee, a pastry, or a helping hand. The results were inspiring. We often fail to truly estimate the reverberation of one act of kindness. One ripple effect creates a tidal wave of love.

When asked how the recipients of the acts of generosity would pay their gift forward, one person shared he would donate clothes to a shelter in downtown Stamford. Another person worked at a country club in Mount Kisco and shared that because of the kindness in Stamford that day, it motivated him to feed the guys working outdoors at the club. One act leads to another and another.

Our dream is to mobilize thousands of people via social media such that at any one moment, we can #elijahmoment and instantaneously people will reach out to another human being. Imagine how different the world could be when harnessed to share our light.

Mark and Ismini Svensson spent their wedding budget to perform one act of kindness in all fifty states. "Social media, whether it's a post or a tweet, can impact your world," Mark says. "It may seem small, but it can go a long way."

The act of kindness may be felt decades later. When I was speaking in New York recently, a woman in the back of the room raised her hand and described the following Elijah moment. She asked me if my mother's name was Sandra. I replied yes, and she then told me she was forever grateful for the hospitality and warmth my mother gave her more than thirty years ago. She had just broken up with a boyfriend in New York and had come to Atlanta for law school at Emory University. She was feeling lonely and went to the synagogue in Atlanta. My parents invited her for a Sabbath meal, and my mother, in particular, befriended her and gave her strength, support, and an emotional boost at a critical juncture in her life. I didn't know her, nor did I remember the event, but here I stood, decades later, learning about an eternal gesture of my mother and her indelible impact on this woman. Wow!

> *"The purpose of life is not to be happy.*
> *It is to be useful, to be honorable, to be*
> *compassionate, to have it make some difference*
> *that you have lived and lived well."*
>
> —Ralph Waldo Emerson

Tool Box

❶ **Create a flash mob of kindness.** Anywhere! Share your progress on our Elijah Moment Facebook page at *https://www.facebook.com/elijahmoment/?ref=hl, #elijahmoment*, and post or share acts of kindness.

❷ **The best gift** (this is a wonderful idea shared by my friends Saul and Mimi): "Mimi and I decided what to do for ourselves for our fiftieth wedding anniversary. We'd been discussing this for a while and were finding it difficult to come to a decision because we found that we really had everything that we wanted. Thank God, there was nothing that we needed. We decided to anonymously include $50 bills in the Kosher Meals on Wheels Thanksgiving package for the twenty indigent people who use this service through the Jewish Federation in the Berkshires. It was one of the best gifts that we ever gave to each other."

❸ **From a ripple to a wave:** Try the following exercise. Think of two blessings in your life for which you are grateful and the source of the act of generosity. Trace the roots. You're the beneficiary of ripples of generosity. Create a wave of kindness. Your appreciation of turning a ripple into a wave will deepen and you'll be inspired.

Peggy Weber Barthold posted on the Elijah Moment Facebook page, "As we look on the street corners, read the paper, or watch the news, there are many who are suffering from hunger and lack of shelter. I keep gallon-size Ziploc baggies in my car filled with healthy, nonperishable food with plastic spoons and warm gloves to hand out if I see a person in need standing on a corner. I just gave a man a bag, and he was so overwhelmed with gratitude. As I drove away I saw him put the gloves on, which made my heart happy. I don't do it for recognition or thanks; I do it because I know there's such a need. I'm blessed with a house, heat, and food, but many are not; maybe think about helping these people who aren't as lucky as we are."

Find Joy in Serving:
The Holiest Night of My Life

We were created to serve. One of the ways I'd motivate my children to do the right thing was to tell them that when they performed a kind act and followed in God's way, their souls would smile. When we open our hearts to others, we feel good inside. It's God's way of letting us know we're on the right track. We spend a lot of money on finding ways to feel good, to experience pleasure. In reality, real and lasting pleasure, the moments when we experience a spiritual high, occur when we live out our purpose. Regardless of our faith tradition, we're all created with the divine spark. This spark (our consciousness, our souls) heats up and burns brighter when we love another.

> *"If a man is called to be a street sweeper,*
> *he should sweep streets even as a Michelangelo*
> *painted, or Beethoven composed music or*
> *Shakespeare wrote poetry. He should sweep streets*
> *so well that all the hosts of heaven and earth*
> *will pause to say, 'Here lived a great street*
> *sweeper who did his job well.'"*
>
> —Martin Luther King Jr.

When we serve, we experience joy. It reveals our purpose and destiny. One of the holiest experiences of my life occurred last summer. My father was undergoing double bypass surgery in Jerusalem. The days before were very unnerving as he reflected on his mortality. He sent me and my siblings a sobering e-mail. I realized the importance of being with him during these fragile moments, and I booked a flight to Jerusalem.

He underwent surgery on a Sunday morning and I arrived in Israel on Monday afternoon after an eleven-hour flight. Within minutes of my arrival, he left the intensive care unit. Although I booked a hotel room near the hospital, upon entering the room, my father asked me to stay with him through the night.

The next twenty-four hours would be some of the most tiring but inspiring moments of my entire life. My father's blood pressure dropped precipitously on a couple of occasions, triggering emergency units; his body temperature cooled and every breath was arduous. I helped him with the most basic tasks.

I left the hospital for about one hour on Tuesday afternoon while my stepmother was with him, to pray at the Western Wall. When I returned, my father, thank God, had stabilized, so I traveled back to the airport and flew home to America. I was in the air more than I was on the ground. My body was exhausted but my soul was on fire.

Growing up, I did my best to honor my parents. I know I could've done more, but I sensed my soul's joy in serving my father. In that instant, I realized the sanctity of the night. Our roles were reversed. He cared for me as a child and now I cared for him. Thank God, he's now on the road to recovery.

In the darkness of the night in Jerusalem, our souls intertwined. His gift of a parent's love for a child and, in turn, my respect and love for him ignited a palpable feeling of joy and purpose that will live in me forever. The experience reinforced within me the counterintuitive role that serving others plays in increasing inner happiness. As Saint Francis of Assisi teaches, "For it is in giving that we receive."

Tool Box

❶ **Stretch your soul:** Whose life will you light today? Write it down and do it. Choose a volunteer activity on a regular basis and stick to it.

❷ **Reframe:** My parents always told me that taking out the garbage wasn't simply bringing the trash bins to the street but an opportunity to honor them. Serving isn't a burden but a blessing. Reframe two acts of service in your life. How does your motivation change?

❸ **Cultivate joy:** Plan a charitable project with your children. They learn from you, and positive feelings are contagious. They'll always remember!

"Joy can only be real if
people look upon their life as a
service and have a definite object in life
outside themselves and their
personal happiness."

—Leo Tolstoy

"Be kind for everyone you meet is fighting
a battle you know nothing about."

—Ian Maclaren,
nineteenth-century Scottish author

Celebrity Stirrings

What if we all agreed to treat everyone we meet going forward as if they were an Elijah?

We all recognize it's a challenge for us. Rather than choosing a reflection from a celebrity for the first "Celebrity Stirrings," I want to celebrate the role of each and every person on Earth, however unsung or ordinary, because everyone possesses a spark of the divine. Whatever a person's background, race, or creed, everyone is a potential Elijah.

Elijah is the child in the classroom. Elijah is the homeless guy on the off ramp with the sign asking for money. Elijah is the maintenance person at your child's school. Elijah is the bus driver, the banker, and the receptionist at the doctor's office. *He is anyone. And he is everyone.* What would the world look like if we all treated one another with the kindness of Elijah? It would be the start of the messianic age.

The spirit of Elijah does exist within our world. Throughout history, many have claimed to meet him. Each story reveals an everyday kindness. Perhaps we've encountered Elijah. Maybe it was Elijah who found your wallet and returned it with all of its contents. Could it have been Elijah that slowed down and waved you on ahead of him in traffic? Maybe it was Elijah at the Stamford Cove.

I'd like to conclude with a story that illustrates a vision and world in which we see the Elijah in others. Once the abbot of a failing monastery went to the local rabbi for advice. He told him there were only five monks left in his order and that they didn't know how to save their beloved institution. "I'm very sorry," the rabbi responded. "But I have no advice for you and your fellow monks. The only thing I know is that one of you is the prophet Elijah."

Back at the monastery, the monks pondered the rabbi's cryptic advice. "Was he saying that one of us is actually Elijah? Who could it be? He must've meant Father Abbot; he's been our leader for so long. Or maybe he meant Brother Thomas. Brother Thomas is certainly a holy man. The rabbi couldn't have meant Brother Elrad. He's just a crotchety old guy. And surely it's not Brother Philip. He's so passive; I barely notice him. But then again, maybe he is Elijah!"

As the monks considered these possibilities, they began to treat one another with extraordinary respect, on the off chance that one of them might actually be Elijah. Slowly, imperceptibly, this aura of extraordinary respect permeated the atmosphere of the monastery and beyond. Now when visitors wandered through the woods, they were drawn to the monastery. They began to bring their friends to show them this special, spiritual place. Gradually, the monastery once again became a center of holiness and light, illuminating the entire town.

Kindness is holiness, the kind of holiness that illuminates our world. Elijah embodies the latent potential in all of us for impact and spiritual greatness. Ask yourself today what you can do to awaken the Elijah within. What difference can you make this year in someone else's life in your houses of worship, your families, your community, or the world?

Ask yourself today how you could change the world by treating everyone as Elijah. Turn to your neighbors and consider how differently you'd see them if you knew they were Elijah and could save the world.

Be the Elijah the world is waiting for and see the Elijah in everyone. Life eternal remains forever. When we forego what is urgent for what is eternal, when we strive to make a difference in a life, we'll build eternity on earth every day of our lives.

"The mystery of human existence lies not in just staying alive, but in finding something to live for."

—*Fyodor Dostoyevsky*,
The Brothers Karamazov

CHAPTER 3

Principle No. 2:
Make Courageous Choices

W hat is a courageous choice? The word "courage" derives
from the Latin root *cor*, which means "heart." A courageous choice is based on inner principles and not
external pressure. A courageous choice emerges from
a steadfast commitment to our values. It is these very decisions that
confront us that reflect the essence of who we are and who we want
to be.

The principle of choosing courageously recognizes the impact of
all our decisions on how we lead our lives now and how we will be
remembered. Oftentimes the route to building character and influence hinges on the choices—both large and small—that we make
every day. Some choices are easier to make than others, and the
weightier ones, those with larger consequences, are often made in

the midst of moral dilemmas. Sometimes it takes courage to make choices that we know will impact not just us but others as well. In this chapter, we'll:

1. Discover the presence of free choice.
2. Anticipate opportunities to make courageous choices.
3. Find inspiration in stories of courage.
4. Learn strategies to develop the ability to make the "right" choices.
5. Develop the self-confidence to draw on our values when confronted with moral dilemmas.
6. See the future impact of our decisions.

What are the three or four most significant decisions you've made in your life? Which choices have given you the greatest pride? When we're confronted with these questions, the first answers that come to mind are the larger events in our lives. We think about a career path, choosing our spouse, or a decision to move to a new area. It's true that these choices affect our lives in significant ways, but when reflecting on the totality of our impact on the world—our existence and legacy—we come to realize that in many cases the seemingly more trivial decisions constitute the essence of who we are and how we'll be remembered.

Take a moment to go back to the eulogy you composed at the end of Chapter 1. Think about the most meaningful eulogies you've heard. What do you remember about them? What character traits speak to a person's reputation? What decisions in life make the most difference in another person's life?

When I sit down with a family to compose a eulogy, I ask the loved ones to focus on the nature of the person. Was he family-oriented? Was she generous of spirit? How would you describe the kind of person he or she was? It's not uncommon for someone to tell me that the deceased never missed a Mets game (hard to believe) or even a Yankees game (more likely) or loved to watch TV, but I try to dig deeper. The family gets it. We get it. We all recognize that Yankee fans or rabid football fans come and go, but the strength of one's character and influence endures forever.

Let's try the following exercise to clarify this principle of making courageous choices. Think of three noble traits, ones to which we all aspire, such as trustworthiness, kindness, and being family-oriented. We may hear at a funeral, "He was a man of his word. You could trust him." Although this is a simple description, its significance is profound.

You may be thinking, *I've heard some pretty exaggerated eulogies filled with stretches and half-truths.* While this may be true, from personal experience, I can tell you that an inauthentic funeral is painful. Furthermore, I'd venture to say that those reading this book are already making a sincere effort to realize their best selves.

After learning about the idea for this book, a close friend of mine commented, "I always wanted a good funeral." What does that mean? Is it only about the way we're remembered or about the way we've lived? Will we be described as trustworthy, kind, and family-oriented? We can't make it up. The answer emerges when we reverse engineer our lives. We'll be known as trustworthy if in every interaction and in every encounter, we did our utmost to be a person others could count on. We'll be known as kind if we can affirm that we rarely spoke ill of others, no matter the temptation. We'll be known as family-oriented if we truly make our families a priority every day.

At one of my weekday classes, this idea hit home when I shared the following conversation. I'd just returned from Sharon Schultz's funeral, the mother of one of our members. She died in her midfifties of cancer and faced her adversity with heroism and faith. The funeral was one of the most moving I've ever experienced. Without consultation, many of the speakers reflected on the woman's motto in life: "There is no one like Him." Despite her illness, she always offered her gratitude to the Almighty and maintained her faith. How did the speakers know what to say? How were they clued in to the same idea? Did she send out a memo from beyond?

I posed this question to my class and added, "What's your motto? Would your children know what to say about you?" One of the people responded, "Well, I guess I could tell them what they should say at my funeral." In an instant, we all realized the foolishness of this answer.

The speakers knew what to say about Sharon Schultz because she lived with such deep faith every day. Throughout her ordeal, she chose to deal with her challenges courageously. Of course, she sought out the best medical team, but she didn't take her family, friends, and medical support team for granted. She found strength in her faith, and rather than focus on her own illness, she harnessed the will to support others faced with similar circumstances. She thanked everyone for their prayers and care for her. One of her friends embroidered Sharon's phrase of faith on her head covering. Sharon sang the words, "There is no one like Him" daily. She is remembered for her inspirational faith and courage because she lived it and people knew it about her. What about us?

In Chapter 1, we designed our own prototype by looking into the future and identifying the core values of our lives, those things for which we want to be remembered. What motto might describe us, as Sharon's motto described her greatest value? You might sum it up by saying, "I want to have a good name and reputation." This is a good aspiration, but gaining it will require having the courage to consistently stand by your convictions and being trustworthy even when it requires sacrifice.

Recently, during a father-son learning session on this topic, one of the fathers shared the following story, which resonates within to this day.

> When I was around ten or eleven, one day a friend and I decided that, as a joke, we'd come up to an old woman who we saw walking in the neighborhood and pretend to ask her silly things that she couldn't possibly understand and know the answer to. The woman was hard of hearing and frail, and her confusion about our questioning was (embarrassingly) amusing to us, so we kept making fun of her. Unbeknownst to me, one of our neighbors saw this encounter and made my parents aware.
>
> My parents were flabbergasted and made two important points that I remember to this day: (1) They asked me how I would like it if some kids treated my own grandmother (with whom I was very close and who was also frail and hard of hearing) the way I had treated this woman; and (2) When I behaved in this manner, I not only ruined my own reputation but the reputation of my parents and the entire family.
>
> As punishment, I had to purchase a few dozen roses with my allowance and stand by the neighborhood supermarket (purposefully a public location) all afternoon handing out individual flowers to every older person I saw. It was a lesson learned and never forgotten.

What do we want our reputation to be? How do our actions reflect on our family, community, and God? One of the wisest sages to grace this earth, Solomon, reflected that a good reputation is more valuable than wealth. He challenges us to ponder what mark we truly want to make in the world. What do we truly want to leave behind?

We live in a world of confusion. We invest our time, energy, and resources in immediate pleasure. Yet when we reverse engineer our lives, we realize that the greatest pleasure lies not in the decisions of convenience but in the words of conviction. One of the core principles of leading a life of deep fulfillment and endurance is our ability to make courageous choices in every moment.

> *"Character is like a tree and reputation*
> *like a shadow. The shadow is what we think*
> *of it; the tree is the real thing."*
>
> —Abraham Lincoln

Foundations

Recently I asked my wife to share a courageous decision. She glanced at me from across the table in the restaurant and answered, "The painter." At first I didn't appreciate the reference. Then she reminded me that when we were getting quotes to have our house painted, we verbally agreed to hire a painter based on his quote, and we did. But after making this agreement, we received another estimate from a different painter that was several thousand dollars less. Although the cost savings was significant, we decided that the price for breaking our word was too high, so we stuck with the original painter. Upon reflection, it was a great example of how often a small decision is truly reflective of the kind of person we aspire to be.

Oprah Winfrey says that "[a]s you become more clear about who you really are, you'll be better able to decide what is best for you—the first time around." As we practice making choices that align with who we want to be and how we want to be remembered when we're gone, we'll gain the fortitude and self-confidence we need when making right choices going forward.

Studies show that most people rarely find the inner strength to make the best choices. When we're afraid of making tough decisions, it often leads to a life of remorse and regret. In a recent book by Australian palliative nurse Bronnie Ware, she notes that the most common regret at the end of one's life is wishing that "I had the courage to live a life true to myself, not the life others expected of me."

When people realize that their life is almost over and look back on it clearly, it's easy to see how many dreams have gone unfulfilled. Most people haven't honored even half of their dreams and have had to die knowing that it was due to choices they had made—or not made.

Two of my close friends are Brian Kriftcher and Rich Vogel. Recently, Rich assumed the presidency of the Stamford Jewish Community Center (JCC). In his acceptance speech, he shared the sources of inspiration for his decision to prioritize the JCC in his life. His choice to take on this communal role emanated from a courageous choice by our close friend Brian. Rich shared:

I feel compelled to share a board meeting moment with you from many years ago because it had such a profound impact on me and many others on the lay leadership side. The scene is late 2006 before the economic meltdown, just on the heels of the Maccabi games, which we hosted. And Brian asks to speak for a minute. And he begins, very seriously, to tell us about a very weighty decision that he's made . . . it's a big one . . . the family deliberated.

Brian says, "I'm going to leave my position at the firm [meaning the very successful hedge fund that he founded] and follow my heart into teaching and toward the service of the community. And, while I'm nervous, I've never been surer of the impact that I want to have and in the pursuit of leaving the world in a better place than I found it." All I could think of was how profound this decision really was. How genuine and in touch it was with those things that are really important in this world; how we as a board and an agency would be well served to embody and model this example. It was a courageous statement born of a passion to serve. I am moved to this day by the power of Brian's spirit and ideals, and the fact that, without wanting to, he has made an indelible impression on me for sure, and I'll bet on others in this room.

Each of us is defined by the things we do every day: the jobs we go to, the people we associate with, the things we spend our time doing. Certainly, Brian appreciated the impact his decision would have on his family, but he couldn't fathom the inspiration it would fuel in others. Think about it for a moment. Brian made a decision; Rich in turn inspired others. Although we may only realize the impact of one decision in hindsight, the awareness of our potential impact with each choice we make heightens the stakes and will give us fuel and motivation to make such decisions now.

Before we go further, I want to clarify another point. When we speak about choices and the dozens we make every day, I'm not referring to choices about the clothes you wear or the food you eat. In hundreds of eulogies that I've written or heard, it's not surprising to hear that the deceased was a dapper dresser or a lover of Italian food. These choices do not represent the essence of who we are or want to be.

Sadly, our most significant choices are often made at Starbucks. In Nora Ephron's film, *You've Got Mail*, Joe Fox reflects, "The whole purpose of places like Starbucks is for people with no decision-making ability whatsoever to make six decisions just to buy one cup of coffee.

Short, tall, light, dark, caf, decaf, low-fat, non-fat, etc. So people who don't know what the hell they're doing or who on earth they are can, for only $2.95, get not just a cup of coffee but an absolutely defining sense of self: Tall. Decaf. Cappuccino."

Here's the truth: We're making hundreds of meaningful choices every day. These small decisions require reservoirs of strength, faith, and clarity. Every day we're blessed with dozens, if not hundreds, of opportunities to make a difference in this world through our choices.

How will you know a courageous choice when you see it?

Do you want to be remembered as a giver or a taker? Do you want to be remembered for your honesty, authenticity, and warmth? These are the moral choices confronting us every day whether in private or in public.

We make a promise; do we get back to someone with an answer? We're asked to help someone; do we seize the chance to help? We're entrusted with confidential information; do we keep a secret? We're exhausted at the end of a hard day; do we smile when we walk into our home and give our family our best?

Every day we're confronted by myriads of moral choices. I believe that we all sense intuitively that the value and worth of a life emerges from our choices, which embody a set of principles and outlook on life, and from a perspective that every moment offers an opportunity for impact.

> *"It is our choices that show what we truly are,*
> *far more than our abilities."*
>
> —J. K. Rowling

Consider the impact of a simple hello or a warm welcome. Have you ever been in a room with hundreds of people yet felt alone? How differently do you feel when someone comes over to you and reaches out to connect with you?

You might be thinking to yourself that choosing to greet someone is not courageous. How about when you're in the midst of your own conversation or in a rush? We may be walking through the supermarket checkout line, texting, answering e-mails, and sliding our credit card without taking a moment to look up to inquire about the cashier's well-being. If so, we've missed a chance to make someone's day!

You may be thinking that this seems trivial. The cashier couldn't care less. But it's not true. When we take the time to move beyond our comfort zone and acknowledge another human being, make eye contact, or invite him or her to sit next to us and begin a conversation, the impact of the encounter may endure forever.

I recently heard an amazing story about a security guard at a meat-packing factory. At the end of the day, the owner asked the security guard to lock the doors and go home. The guard believed that there was someone still inside. The owner argued that everybody was gone, but the guard sensed differently. He decided to do a walk-through and discovered that one of the workers was locked in the meat freezer. As he opened the door to let him out, the owner couldn't help but ask, "How did you know? There are hundreds of workers here. How did you know that he was still in the factory?"

The man responded, "Although there are hundreds of workers that come in and out every day, this worker is the only one that stops to say hello in the morning and good evening at night. I missed his greeting, so I knew he was still inside."

Imagine the power of one kind word. How can we identify and anticipate such moments?

They emerge from an appreciation of free choice. Most of us are not victims to our surroundings. Every day we wake up, we're charged with a responsibility to affirm life. Every moment we're given two paths to follow and we're challenged with a chance to either elevate our lives and the world around us or not. A choice not taken is also a choice.

The Almighty invests all of us with the spirit and strength each day to harness this inner power. The question is whether we cherish the gift of free choice to express our deepest values or live on cruise control and make decisions out of convenience and not conviction.

We really do have free choice for life's important decisions. Each of us possesses within us a divine voice that calls on us, motivates us, and inspires us to be our very best. If we want to make good choices in life, we need to understand that the more soulful choices we make, the easier making such decisions will be in the future.

The Momentum Factor

One positive, life-affirming choice inherently energizes us to make further such choices in the future. For instance, if someone is raised with the value of honesty and is given the chance to cheat to get ahead, he may deliberate about the cost of his transgression. Is it worth it? If he overcomes this temptation, the next time it will be easier to withstand the pressure because he has developed the inner fortitude.

If I have one hundred dollars to give to charity, should I give that amount a single time or a dollar for the next hundred days? Jewish mystics say that it is better to give a smaller amount over an extended period of time, since it will habituate us to making the right choices.

As one act of courage buttresses us with the will to do more, conversely, the smallest compromise will often be the first crack in our character that leads to a much larger fissure in our moral armor. The first time we fail to listen to that voice, it is hard. With each compromise, we think less about our decision and become inured to follow what *feels* good as opposed to what *is* good. As the old saying goes, we tend to fall in the direction we're leaning.

> *"It takes twenty years to build a*
> *reputation and five minutes to ruin it.*
> *If you think about that, you'll do*
> *things differently."*
>
> —Warren Buffett

Listen to the "final" words of Peregrine Financial Group chief executive Russell Wasendorf Sr., which he penned in a suicide attempt note. In his letter, he confessed to bilking customers out of $200 million: "I had no access to additional capital and I was forced into a difficult decision: Should I go out of business or cheat? I guess my ego was too big to admit failure. So I cheated; I falsified the very core of the financial documents of PFG, the bank statements."

One choice altered his destiny. I can guarantee you that headlines about cases like this one are merely the culmination of small decisions that spiraled out of control. One compromise leads to the next. Lives are ruined and the fallout shakes the foundations of our families, businesses, government, and schools.

In stark contrast, one of the most respected financiers in the world, Steve Schwarzman, CEO of Blackstone, the largest hedge fund in the world, shared with me his unwavering dedication to building a firm rooted in honesty and ethics: "When I interview new recruits to the firm, I warn them that if even only once they engage in behavior that smells wrong, not only will I fire them but I will ruin them, prosecute them, and destroy them. When asked by my partners why I am so harsh, I explain that I want everyone in my firm to be deeply rooted in doing the right thing. Your integrity is only tested when it costs you something."

What happens when no one is looking? How are we guided when only we will know the impact of our actions? These moments, when all we can hear is our own inner voice, are fertile ground for making truly courageous choices.

The summer 2012 Olympic swimming meet was such a battlefield of moral indecision. The question for the swimmers was whether to use the dolphin kick, an illegal maneuver, beyond the first few feet of the race. In a *New York Times* article exploring this topic, some swimmers admitted to using this kick to gain an edge. They knew that it was virtually impossible to be caught. "After all," commented one swimmer, "everyone is pushing the rules and pushing the boundaries, and if you're not doing it, you're not trying hard enough."

Yet one swimmer, American bronze medalist Brendan Hansen, got it. He remarked, "There was never a thought in my head that the extra dolphin kick or two was something I was going to do. I was not raised to cheat. It's not something I practice." Hansen realized that a truly great life is not one guided by external regulation but by inner motivation. He remarked that he wouldn't exploit loopholes in the rules, that it was "each athlete's choice but they will have to live with it for the rest of their lives."[1]

Do we possess such courage with our own convictions? One split-second decision defines us, embodies us, and is how we'll be remembered. Every week in the news, we see examples of the truism that a reputation is built over a lifetime, but one moral indiscretion destroys one. Thousands of years before social media, the Ethics of the Fathers taught, "Do not say something we do not want to be heard, for in the end it will be heard." No action is private. Every choice reflects our past and determines our future.

Winston Churchill remarked, "The power of man has grown in every sphere, except over himself." Almost all of our critical decisions in life emerge from a deeply personal tug-of-war. We're all alone except for our inner voice. It whispers to us to be the best we can be and rise to the moment. Can you hear it? It beckons inside you right now. If you listen carefully, you can sense it pushing up and saying, "You have so much to live for. You can make a difference every day. Be strong and courageous. You will leave a mark in this world now and forever."

Nourish your inner voice and amplify its sound and significance in your life.

> *"It is not hard to make decisions when*
> *you know what your values are."*
>
> —Roy Disney

In the heat of a decision we may be internally conflicted. Do we succumb to external pressures or draw on internal principles?

Strategies

No. 1: Remember Who You Are

These four words symbolize my anchor in life. As a teenager on my way to party with friends or alone for the first time as a freshman in college, I always tried to remember this motto from my parents. We only live in a cocoon for so long. As parents, we'll not always be available to guide our children as they grow older. We hope that we instill the values for them to remain rooted and confident in their beliefs. When no one is looking and when no one is regulating our behavior, we must remember who we are.

Who are you? What are the values that define you? Spend some time reflecting on these questions. Only when you know your values can you live them. If we search for approval or accolades prior to making a small decision, we won't be prepared for what could be a truly transformative decision. We won't possess the strength to express our deepest beliefs and aspirations. Our lives are, in fact, constituted by the heartfelt choices we make every day.

I'm reminded of the story in *Ah, but Your Land Is Beautiful* by South African writer Alan Paton. He tells of a man who died and came before God. "Where are your wounds?" asks God. "I have none," said the man. "Why?" responds God, "was there nothing worth fighting for?"

Which beliefs of yours are worth fighting for?

Tool Box

❶ Identify three core values in your life.

❷ Reflect on three courageous choices driven by your values in your personal, work, and communal life.

❸ Describe an experience when one of your values was challenged and you fought to uphold it.

No. 2: You're the Link in the Chain

The Bible speaks of Joseph's heroic choice when he was tempted by Potiphar's wife in ancient Egypt. You may know the story from the Broadway show *Joseph and the Amazing Technicolor Dreamcoat*. Joseph was one of the handsomest men around, and Potiphar's wife couldn't take her hands off him. It was just her and him, all alone, with nobody else at home—the perfect opportunity. Yet at the last minute, Joseph courageously withstood her temptations. In history he's known forever as "Joseph the Righteous One" for this heroic act (and believe me, running away cost him). What gave him the strength to withstand the temptations? The mystics teach that the critical moment was when he conjured up the image of his father. He understood the stakes of his decision. Sure, it would feel good now, but his family was counting on him to uphold the traditions with which he was raised. In *Divine Comedy*, Dante wrote, "The hottest places in Hell are reserved for those who in a time of moral crisis preserve their neutrality."

You're a link to the past and a bridge to the future. When you reverse engineer your life, you become aware of the reverberations of your actions. What would your parents say? How will your children remember you? Previous generations and ones not yet born are counting on you. You're the link in the chain.

Tool Box

❶ **How do you remain connected to your past even when nobody is looking?**

❷ **Identify a past and present moral dilemma in your life** and chart the future impact of making a courageous or convenient decision.

❸ **Who motivates you to want to be your best?** A partner, a child, a parent? Keep them in your mind's eye.

No. 3: The Jockey and the Horse

Jewish mysticism teaches that every human being consists of two inclinations. The first is our inner voice calling us to be our best and the second urges us to follow the path of immediate gratification. This internal struggle is the battlefield of courageous choices. As shared earlier, the choices may be minor ones, but our decisions reflect the strength of our character. Think for a moment of our aspirations as the jockey and our temptations as the horse. The critical question is who is leading whom at the point of choice. Are we leading the horse and choosing courageously, or is the horse leading us down the path of least resistance? Train yourself to be the jockey and master the moment.

Tool Box

❶ **Spend five minutes every night identifying two conscious choices you made during the day.** Evaluate whether you were the jockey or the horse. Analyze how you can do better tomorrow.

❷ **Give a minimum of five cents to a charity of your choice every day and choose a text for five minutes of daily study to sharpen your spiritual senses.**

❸ **Build your self-confidence.** What choice in the past week gave you the greatest inner fulfillment? What conditions contributed to your ability to make that choice? How can you harness these lessons for the future? Name an upcoming opportunity.

No. 4: Holy Habits

My battlefield is different from yours. What may be challenging for me may be different for you. Through the practice of self-discipline, we'll be fortified to make more thoughtful and principled choices. Each good decision moves our moral pivot point and makes future ethical decisions even easier.

When we develop this habit, we'll be fortified to make the "right" choices throughout our lives, and we'll leave this world not only without regrets but we'll know we did our best with our finest efforts and essence.

When you're confronted with a moment of indecision, with only a split second to decide whether to listen to your inner voice, you'll follow what you're conditioned to do. Develop holy habits. One good choice energizes another.

Tool Box

❶ **When you wake up, name a good deed you'll do today.**

❷ **Never keep extra change from a cashier**—always return it.

❸ **Don't be a bystander.** Pick up a lost object; help a stranger or friend in need.

No. 5: Celebrate Small Victories

Our lives aren't measured by how many touchdowns we score but by how far we move the ball. When we die, we won't be judged against someone else's life but against our own potential. Did we do the best we could with the hand we were dealt?

Celebrate the singles and the doubles. The small moral victories will constitute an enduring and memorable legacy. Those choices will determine whether we'll be remembered as greedy or generous, honest or deceitful, self-serving or selfless. We must never forget that even if we stumble, and we will, tomorrow is a new day. Each morning we're blessed with an opportunity to choose life and get back on the road to success.

Tool Box

❶ Write down two decisions in the past week that gave you inner peace.

❷ Express your gratitude to someone else for the blessings they bring into your life.

❸ Say "thank you" to the cashier while looking him or her in the eye.

Choosing courageously not only reflects our ethics but our ethos for living life with optimism and gratitude. In the final analysis, we're endowed with the gift of free choice to embrace our divine voice inside and elevate and energize the people we encounter every day of our lives.

"I never saw him without a smile." Will they say that about you? Every expression leaves an impact. Do we wallow in our own misery or uplift another soul and touch the world? When we walk in the door, do we give our children a hug and a warm greeting? We're all role models. Our values are not taught but caught.

Although Shakespeare wrote so eloquently, "All the world is a stage," I prefer to quote the great baseball player Joe DiMaggio. He was once asked late in his career why he still ran out to center field at the end of each inning. After all, he had nothing left to prove. He'd won a number of MVPs and World Series rings. He answered with words that ring so true: "I always hustle because I never know whether there may be one young fan in the stands that day who has never seen me play before. I want to make sure that he knows the real Joe DiMaggio."

At every moment of our lives, whether young or old, we're called up to be our very best. We're charged with living life with passion and purpose. The world is watching. If we choose courageously and optimize our opportunities, we'll know that we gave of our gifts, touched the world, and lived our lives in a way that we'll be remembered in blessed memory.

Celebrity Stirrings

Senator Joseph Lieberman was a senior senator from Connecticut and the first Jewish candidate for vice president. As a statesman who observes the Sabbath, he does his best to remain loyal to his faith while committed to his country. Furthermore, throughout his career, he's been known for his independent thinking. Often he crossed party lines for his beliefs. In a recent interview reflecting on his choices, he commented, "When I decide a course of action, it is not for fear of failure. If I lose because I stood for my beliefs, I will always be at peace. I never want to be remembered for playing life safe. I want to be remembered for doing what was right."

Throughout his career, Senator Lieberman exhibited not only a firm commitment to his political principles but also his faith. Despite his national office, he observed the sanctity of the Sabbath. He shared one of his most unforgettable Sabbath experiences with me, and it also serves as a shining example of his character and courage. It occurred while he was running as the Democratic candidate for vice president. On Friday, December 7, 2000, the Florida Supreme Court ruled for a vote recount in the presidential election. He shared with me that when presidential candidate Al Gore called him with the news, he explained that once sunset arrived, he would be inaccessible via phone, BlackBerry, and other social media until Saturday evening. As the senator shared, "If anyone really needs us, they know how to get us." Moments before the Sabbath arrived, Al called Joe and his wife, Hadassah, and invited them to spend the Sabbath at the vice president's private residence. As the Sabbath was moments away, the senator told me that he could no longer drive to their home, so he and Hadassah, accompanied by Al and his wife, Tipper, walked the mile to the vice presidential home with the Secret Service discreetly walking behind them and security cars at the front and back. I probed further and asked the senator about the roots of his deep and abiding commitment to his faith. He shared with me a courageous choice he made as a college student at Yale University. Although he grew up Sabbath-observant, he stopped observing it for a while. During law school, his grandmother, a warm and loving woman, passed away. She was his connection to faith and the Orthodox tradition. When she passed away, he shared, "I experienced a feeling that now that she was gone, the chain in Jewish history was no longer there and that I now had a choice to put myself in the chain and be part of the future. I was compelled to return." It was this courageous choice as a college student that defined his life and forged his faith and his future.

CHAPTER 4

Principle No. 3:
Seize Meditative Moments

"Nowhere can a man find a quieter retreat
than in his own soul."

—Marcus Aurelius

D eep inside each of us reside the ingredients for a meaningful and fulfilling life. The question is whether we heed
this power and voice. It's hard, given the hectic pace of
every day and the demands of our jobs and families.
Yet if we can find the sacred space to pause, we can rediscover our
purpose.

I learned this lesson years ago while sitting in solitude at a hotel
in Pennsylvania. As a participant in a rabbinic leadership program

with several dozen rabbis across denominations, we were asked at the outset of the seminar to "lock" ourselves in our rooms for three hours to create a visual map of our lives, capturing—in symbols, drawings, and color—our past, present, and future. Those three hours in Philadelphia reignited my personal odyssey and motivated me to reverse engineer my life.

At first I wondered why we'd been asked to break up our newly formed group. But in short order, I realized the wisdom of the plan. While in my room, I thought deeply about my roots, my heritage, my family, my gifts, and my mission in the world. I drew symbols of my past stretching back to the story of Creation, the Revelation on Mount Sinai, and my ancestors, and charted a vision of my future. After our quiet time, we regathered and posted and shared our soul maps. The process renewed my faith in infinite potential.

I share this story with you because it represents the heart and soul of truly embracing the practice of reverse engineering your life. The longest distance in life is between our heads and our hearts. Spiritual success requires developing the training to transform our intentions into reality. We all experience flashes of inspiration when we awake from our spiritual slumber. In those moments, we embrace a seriousness of purpose and pledge to truly devote ourselves to our deepest values. Yet all too often our motivation is short-lived. Soon enough, we're back to old habits.

There is no shortage of people who aspire to growth and greatness. Life is filled with unfulfilled dreams and unrealized potential. As Henry David Thoreau reflected, "Most men lead lives of quiet desperation and go to the grave with the song still in them." You're reading this book because you don't want to follow this path. You don't want to wait for that wake-up call to embrace a life of purpose.

You want to align your body and soul and lead life with urgency and a higher purpose. You have a song within you to sing.

How can you unlock your latent potential within?

The most important principle in ensuring your long-term growth is crafting the time and possessing the tenacity to seize meditative moments. Find the time to turn off the outside world and turn on your inner world. The only way to stay true to who you really are and want to be is through taking the time to step back from the busyness of day-to-day life and reflect on the arc of your spiritual progress. Are you living out your higher purpose or allowing each day to blur into the next?

The journey to reverse engineer your life requires leading a disciplined life. It necessitates carving out time for reflection to review your aspirations, goals, and progress. Seizing meditative moments beckons you to reorient your priorities.

All the good intentions in the world won't translate into action if we don't pause to reflect on our life direction and purpose. If we don't, it could turn out that all of our investments of time, money, love, and talents were for naught.

There's a wonderful story about a high school coach who took his students out to the running track. The coach led the students to the starting line. As the teens stretched into position, the coach called out for them to start. The students took off on their race around the track. The fastest runner strained to keep ahead of the others. As they neared the finish line, one runner pulled ahead and came in first. The others followed as quickly as they could. One runner, though, lagged far behind the others. He finished last by a wide margin.

The coach gathered all the students together. He then declared the slowest student to be the winner, the recipient of the prize. The one who'd finished first, in a burst of frustration, called out, "That isn't fair!

I won the race. I was fastest. I finished first. The student you declared winner was the slowest runner, finishing last."

The coach responded, "In this race, the winner was the one who finished last."

The first-place runner and the rest of the class were unsettled by this answer. They'd always been taught that winning a race meant coming in first. Now the coach had turned the rules upside down. The coach said, "We don't ever know who wins unless we first know what the rules are. If the rules of this particular race were different from what you had assumed, then you have a problem."

Who wins or who loses the race depends on the definition of the rules.

Marc Angel, in his book *Losing the Rat Race, Winning at Life*, writes: "We human beings are placed on earth to attain transcendent treasures—wisdom, love, spiritual insight, moral courage. If we can keep our lives focused on these goals and if we can direct our lives according to these ideals—then we 'win' at life. But if we come to ascribe greater value to mundane attainments—wealth, power, fame—then we may find ourselves having accumulated things that are ultimately of little worth. Winning at life means keeping focused on what is truly important and not getting sidetracked by external glitz. Winning is not a one-time event, but an ongoing way of life."[2]

Remember that the ultimate achievement of happiness, and to truly be remembered, is to strive to lead meaningful lives, to appreciate every day, and to reorient our priorities. Abraham Lincoln said, "I am not bound to win, but I am bound to be true; I am not bound to succeed, but I am bound to live up to the light I have." What are the rules that guide your life? How do you define success? What steps can you take to "win" and achieve inner success and fulfillment?

All too often we reserve serious introspection for the realm of money and health but not our spiritual lives. In the world of business, we'd never think of running a company without setting benchmarks and conducting consistent data analysis. What are our expenses, debt, market share, and profit? Without evaluation, we'll never know whether we're profitable and, more important, how we need to adjust our business model and realign our business practice with our company's purpose. Building a profitable venture or advancing in our career requires focus and daily review.

Beyond the arena of money, we spend a lot of time, for good reason, on our health. Advancements in technology have increased our ability to monitor our bodies. From blood pressure, body mass, and fat percentage to macronutrients, we're focused on optimizing our health. As a friend who wears a body tracker once confessed to me, "I often eat mindlessly, and the Fitbit engages me to be aware of how I treat my body. How much food do I consume? How far have I walked? What is the impact of my caloric intake?"

But do we pay the same amount of attention to our spiritual lives? We're living longer due to greater health consciousness and advancements in medicine and, in fact, the pursuit of health is holy. But in the realm of the spirit, we all too often fail to harness the same resources, time, and focus.

How can you harness the gift of life for maximal impact and fulfillment? You can begin by leading your life as a reflection of your innermost values. The only way to accomplish this goal is *not to wait for external stimuli to jolt you into action but to cultivate an ongoing mechanism to keep your ideal self front and center.*

The principle of seizing meditative moments will enable you to realize your infinite potential. In this chapter we'll explore:

1. How to discover and heed your inner voice.
2. Learn to listen to and appreciate the sounds of silence.
3. Understand the secret of the Sabbath.
4. Acquire meaningful mindfulness.
5. Learn sacred strategies for seizing meditative moments.

Are you ready? Right now, turn off your computer, smartphone, and any other device, and be fully present so you can learn how to seize meditative moments in your life!

Foundations

Discovering and Hearing Your Inner Voice

The secret to seizing meditative moments emerges from the belief that we each possess within us an inner voice, compass, and guide that reflects a higher power and purpose. I know it may sound strange, but each of us is born with this inner voice. It's implanted from conception. It's a divine homing device that yearns to unleash light, love, and impact in the world. It's the "still, small voice" that is strong and resonant, calling on us to pursue what is right and purposeful in our lives. The voice reminds us of who we are and who we are destined to be.

From personal experience, I know this reality to be true. I've heard it, and you likely have, too, in various moments in your life. When have you heard it?

I want to challenge you. Whether you're a believer in a higher power or not, we all know deep down that life has purpose. We want to make a difference in the time we are here. The following scenario speaks to the universality of this quest and search within all of us. The voice is there.

Imagine the ecstasy of being alive moments after being in mortal danger. Imagine the experience of being drawn under the waves in the ocean until almost losing consciousness and then breaking the surface and gasping a lifesaving breath of air. In that moment, you possess a super consciousness of being alive. In that instant, you are fully cognizant that your life was in the balance.

Some might call it God or a holy spark inside; some might say it's our consciousness. Regardless, the voice declares that we are born into this world for a mission. In the broadest terms, we're here to serve the Almighty. Life possesses a purpose. You're not a random collection of molecules. You experience joy, guilt, love, sadness, hope, and the boundless and ever-flowing yearning to leave this world a better place for having lived in it. When we recognize this voice, this fire inside, and it animates our daily lives, we soar. When we experience it, we know it to be true. In the words of theologian and author Frederick Buechner, "The place God calls you to be is the place where your deep gladness and the world's deep hunger meet."

Rabbi Moshe Hayyim Luzzatto, in his seminal work *The Path of the Just*, echoes this idea in his first chapter, entitled "Man's Duty in His World," when he states: "In truth, the essential completeness of mankind is achieved in attaching oneself to God."[3] This is the foundation of life.

Every moment in which we do not cling to a higher power, we're not complete. We're all charged with infusing the physical and temporal with eternity and holiness. In these moments and in this awareness, we're truly alive! The amount of time we remember our purpose in life is the amount of time we're living life at the highest level. As Eleanor Roosevelt shared, "The purpose of life is to live it, to taste experience to the utmost, to reach out eagerly and without fear for newer and richer experience."

When we experience every day without an awareness of our purpose, we're deadened to life. It becomes a semblance of death. We need to revive ourselves every day and every hour. When we perform a good deed, we should remember that the goal isn't simply the performance but the ignition of our inner pilot light. Each person possesses a spark of the divine—the soul—that compels our quest for meaning and significance. The more we align our thoughts and actions with nourishing this life, the more alive we will feel.

Mindlessness without mission is like a body without a soul. It's no wonder the Danish philosopher Søren Kierkegaard wrote, "Boredom is the root of all evil." When we're not living in an awareness of the moment, life becomes a blur, and we meander aimlessly through it. But each new day is a day for a revival of the dead. Every day our souls can sing. We can lead life on a higher frequency.

You may be wondering: *Do I have a voice inside of me that will arise to ignite my quest for meaning in life?* The answer is a resounding "Yes!" Every human being, regardless of our faith tradition, possesses an innate homing device for holiness. We are divinely designed for spiritual greatness. Deep down we all know this is true. For this reason, in the crisis situations in our lives, when the shell of numbness to our inner fire is broken, we're able to hear it; we feel it and we yearn to live by it.

> *"What is a soul? It's like electricity—*
> *we don't really know what it is, but it's a*
> *force that can light a room."*
>
> —Ray Charles

Our souls possess the spiritual DNA for our life success and fulfillment. A lifetime of effort and soulful living will help us realize our divine potential. When we invest in our potential, we bring our innate wisdom to reality, and our souls sing. We experience an unbridled joy that we're living out our life purpose. We recognize these moments because we're programmed this way. It's for this reason that the process of reverse engineering your life reflects the real you and your innate desire. I'm not asking you to be somebody you're not but to peel back the barriers so you can become the person you truly want to be.

There's a common saying that "There are no atheists in foxholes." When we confront our mortality, we cannot help but heed our inner voice. This dramatic encounter can be heartening or haunting, depending on the life we lead, and it's most acute on a person's deathbed.

Jewish mysticism teaches that the sensation of death can be compared to one of two metaphors: taking hair out of milk or thorns out of a bush. One is easy and the other is painful. When a person leads a life defined by the pursuit of physical pleasure, it's painful to die. On the final day, he or she sees the truth, hears the inner voice, and realizes the folly of their investments, for the body is dying and will not live on. They experience deep regret for not prioritizing life in a soulful way. On a deeper level, the soul doesn't want to leave, for we (the soul) realize that we could've and should've done more.

Many years ago, I visited a man I knew at a remote hospice in central Connecticut. He had a couple of adult children and a few grandchildren but no one was there with him. It was one of the saddest moments I've experienced. I entered the stark and empty room where he lay all alone. As I held his hand and offered words of strength as he embarked on his journey to the next world, I sensed in him a feeling of remorse. Where was his family? He'd never wanted his life to end this way. I did my best to offer strength to him as I recited the confessional prayer, but as I left, I had this lingering feeling that he was alone.

In contrast, one of the most uplifting images is when I arrive at the hospital and the person who is dying is surrounded by family. Words of love and songs of strength are shared. There's a distinct feeling in the room that despite the impending death of the person, he'll live on in his family, friends, and everyone he's touched.

Each of us possesses an inner voice beckoning us and pushing us toward greatness. Regardless of our background, economic strata, or faith, implanted inside is a higher power serving as our anchor, compass, and energizer throughout life.

When do you hear this voice? Are you conscious of its resonance and relevance every day?

The more we lead our lives in tune with this higher frequency, the more fulfilled our lives will be now and forever. The image of death is not intended to be depressing but as a stirring reminder of the brevity of life and the awesome responsibility we all share to eternalize every moment and sanctify every encounter.

You're reading this book because you truly want to make the most of your life. The passage of time creeps up all too quickly, and we rarely maximize all of our opportunities to prioritize the significant in our lives before the urgent. God willing, in the course of reverse engineering your life, you'll be motivated to adopt the transformative principles introduced throughout the chapters of this book. How do we ensure that these flashes of inspiration don't recede to the annals of time? How do we remain committed to the pursuit of personal growth?

*"It is not that we have so little
time but that we lose so much. . . .
The life we receive is not short but we make
it so; we are not ill provided but use
what we have wastefully."*

—Seneca, *On the Shortness of Life*

The Sounds of Silence

The most essential element in reverse engineering your life is seizing your meditative moments. It's about not waiting for a crisis to happen to awaken your inner voice but crafting ongoing moments of reflection daily.

A story is told about a farmer who misplaced a valuable watch somewhere in his barn. He asked everyone to search up and down to find his precious heirloom. Unfortunately, despite hours spent looking for the timepiece, it was nowhere to be found. Later in the day, a young boy announced to the farmer with great joy that he had found the watch. Astonished, the farmer asked the boy how he was able to find it even though so many others had searched high and low without finding it. The boy responded, "Well, once the barn was quiet, I put my head to the ground and heard the watch ticking." We may only hear our inner voice when we turn off the outside world.

*"I have spent many days stringing and
unstringing my instrument while the song
I came to sing remains unsung."*

—Rabindranath Tagore

We live in a world bombarded by noise. Wherever we go, we're confronted by sounds and sights vying for our attention. Drivers are often distracted, and it's not uncommon to be interrupted during dinner by our personal devices. Sitting in front of our computers, we have trouble staying focused. We experience a jolt of joy when we receive texts and when our posts are liked on Facebook. We run from place to place, seemingly accomplishing more but in reality thinking less.

Do you walk in the dark or in the light? Is your day aimless or purposeful? Do you react to events or create your own destiny?

"The human race is a monotonous affair.
Most people spend the greatest part of their time
working in order to live, and what little freedom
remains so fills them with fear that they seek
out any and every means to be rid of it."

—Goethe, *The Sorrows of Young Werther*

Develop the discipline to create the sacred space needed to nourish the stirrings of your soul. How can you discover your meditative moment? The most important ingredient is silence, when you turn off the outside world and turn on your inner world. It can't happen amid the daily cacophony of sounds. In the silence and quiet, we can't help but hear the whispers of our soul. In the words of Mother Teresa, "In the silence of the heart God speaks. If you face God in prayer and silence, God will speak to you. Then you will know that you are nothing. It is only when you realize your nothingness, your emptiness, that God can fill you with Himself. Souls of prayer are souls of great silence." When was the last time you truly experienced silence? How did you feel? What emotions were awakened? Silence is all too rare in modern times.

To borrow a slogan from Coca-Cola, this principle is about the pause that refreshes. The more we reflect on our lives, the more fulfilled our lives will be, and thus aligned with our deepest aspirations. A walk in the woods or communing with nature may stir our senses and encourage us to return to our roots.

Chuck Leavell, a founding member of the Allman Brothers Band and a longtime touring member of the Rolling Stones, lives on a farm in Georgia and credits his grounding as a rock and roller to his connection to the earth. It was the inspiration for founding Mother Nature Network, an online network of news on the environment. When speaking with Chuck, he reflected, "Ralph Waldo Emerson once said, 'In the woods, we return to reason and faith.' I think that's so true. I think America and perhaps many parts of the world have somehow lost their connection with the land. It is sad and dangerous. That is how I got hooked on the environment. To be able to be involved in Mother Nature Network is very, very special for me. The silence awakened within me a renewed sense of potential and life purpose. It was a gift to reorient my life around my most cherished values and dreams."

Seizing our meditative moments enables us to lead our lives in perfect alignment with our inner, transcendent desires. These "pauses"—great and small, daily, weekly, or monthly—serve as the anchor for recalibration.

The options for seizing a meditative moment range from prayer, walking, yoga, or simply being alone and apart from the noise of daily life. The strategies are personal and plentiful, and we'll explore some of them in this chapter, but the critical component is frequency and fidelity to the process.

The Power of One Moment

Never forget that any minute of the day can be channeled for growth and greatness. The challenge, though, is that we rarely know up front the eternal significance of a moment. We travel through time not a minute at a time but days and years at a time. Life becomes a blur. As time passes, we wonder where the time has gone. We think, *What have I accomplished?*

Moments are as numerous as the stars in the sky, and any one of them could prove to be the most significant of our lives. However mundane a moment may appear, the miraculous may be waiting to be unwrapped within. Intellectually, each of us realizes that sometimes a moment can change our lives when we least expect it. Perhaps the moment comes when we meet a new person or experience the divine in the world. Seizing meditative moments is not only about the deliberate, sacred spaces we craft for reflection but about being open to realizing that inspiration may flow at any moment.

I reflected with my father on the spiritual roots of his devotion to a life infused with spirit, and he told me that he experienced an epiphany as a young boy while staying at a youth camp. While singing during the Sabbath service, he felt moved to the core, and as he described it, "It added fuel to a fire inside that yearned to break free." He didn't know the impact of that moment in advance, but he was receptive to experiencing it and letting it penetrate his soul.

As a father, I think about the times I sit around the table on the Sabbath and the sacred time to connect with family and friends. We never know where our conversation will go, but it's not uncommon to engage in thoughtful dialogue about life, sharing events in our week that enriched our relationships and deepened our perception of the divine in our lives. Realizing that any moment can be one of growth is the first step. *Be receptive.*

Two obstacles often stand in our way: Paul McCartney and Annie. We're caught with Paul in the past and captivated by Annie in the future. Paul sings, "Yesterday, all my troubles seemed so far away, now it looks as though they're here to stay, oh, I believe in yesterday." We're held captive by mistakes of the past and don't have the courage to move forward. How many of us have spent time reflecting on moments lost in regret and opportunities lost? Time spent in the past is exactly that: moments lost.

On the other hand, how many of us spend time dreaming of the future, looking toward a moment to come? As Annie sings, "Tomorrow, tomorrow, I love you, tomorrow, you're only a day away." Every day is focused on anticipating the future instead of living in the present.

The moment we must seize right now is the one in front of us. It's not easy. We live in a generation that has many distractions. Even when we try to be focused on the day—today—we're affected by CPA: not certified public accounting but a syndrome I call "continuous partial attention." We pay continuous partial attention in an effort not to miss anything—multitasking, surfing the Web, answering our cell phones—yet in the end, we gain nothing.

I was privy to a conversation describing a person who was ill. One person commented to his friend, "Did you know he had to have two fingers amputated?" The listener responded, "That's nice." A second later, the listener realized he wasn't really focused on the conversation and quickly expressed his empathy, but this interchange is only one example of many in which we're not focused and living in the moment—*today.*

One of the most important life lessons I ever learned was from my speech teacher in college. He spoke about the importance of compartmentalizing one's mind. If when I'm at work my mind is at home, and if when I'm home my mind is at work, I'm nowhere. I'll accomplish little in life by being nowhere. Being present is one of the most powerful tools you'll discover in life.

When you're speaking to someone, be fully engaged. When you're outside, be fully present in the beauty and the moment. While in college, I studied this poem by Gerard Manley Hopkins, which embodies the reservoir of inspiration present every day.

THE WORLD IS CHARGED WITH THE GRANDEUR OF GOD.
IT WILL FLAME OUT, LIKE SHINING FROM SHOOK FOIL;
IT GATHERS TO A GREATNESS, LIKE THE OOZE OF OIL
CRUSHED. WHY DO MEN THEN NOW NOT RECK HIS ROD?
GENERATIONS HAVE TROD, HAVE TROD, HAVE TROD;
AND ALL IS SEARED WITH TRADE; BLEARED, SMEARED WITH TOIL;
AND WEARS MAN'S SMUDGE AND SHARES MAN'S SMELL: THE SOIL
IS BARE NOW, NOR CAN FOOT FEEL, BEING SHOD.

AND FOR ALL THIS, NATURE IS NEVER SPENT;
THERE LIVES THE DEAREST FRESHNESS DEEP DOWN THINGS;
AND THOUGH THE LAST LIGHTS OFF THE BLACK WEST WENT
OH, MORNING, AT THE BROWN BRINK EASTWARD, SPRINGS —
BECAUSE THE HOLY GHOST OVER THE BENT
WORLD BROODS WITH WARM BREAST AND WITH AH!
BRIGHT WINGS.

We experience the divine all the time—every morning when the sky is ablaze with orange yellow rays, at sunset when the splendor of the moment so dazzles us that our minds give pause and take us to a higher reality. These are moments when we discover the divine in the world and glimpse the eternal.

In truth, God's presence is everywhere, but it's so well disguised that often we miss it completely. In fact, as Eckhart Tolle writes in the *Power of Now*, "if you know where to look, you will find it everywhere. A portal opens up every moment."

The Bible's story of Hagar and Ishmael illustrates this truth. Hagar was in the desert and bereft of food. She turned to God for help, and the Bible records that she opened her eyes and miraculously saw a well of water in the middle of the barren plain. Pay careful attention to the choice of words. The usual word for open is "Vayiftach": "and she opened," but in this case, the Torah uses "Vayifkach," or "she gained wisdom and understanding." Here the Torah is teaching a profound idea. The well didn't miraculously appear out of nowhere; the well was always there. The water was always there. God was ever-present. However, she couldn't see it. It remained hidden from her until a moment of insight when she realized that the blessing was right in front of her very eyes.

How many times do we ignore the blessings in front of our eyes—our spouses, children, families, and the world—simply because we're not in the moment?

Most of us recognize that we're charged by God with fulfilling our unique mission in the world using our God-given talents. However, the mystics teach an idea even *more* extraordinary. They believe that we each have a divine destiny every *moment* of our lives. We're called upon to live out our destiny every moment of every day. King David writes in the Psalms, "Today, hearken to my voice." God calls upon us to live in the moment and actualize the once-in-a-lifetime opportunity we face today at this moment. We'll never have this moment again!

I believe that we *can* turn moments missed into moments maximized. We just need to know where to look and what to anticipate. What if we could identify a moment filled with potential and endless possibilities? What if we knew that there was a moment coming when we would meet God in a way that would change our lives forever? How would we treat that moment? How would we identify it?

Author, pastor, and filmmaker Erwin McManus writes, "There are few things more powerful than a life lived with passionate clarity. Every moment is waiting to be seized by those who are chasing daylight." Seizing these meditative moments is living a life in which you're chasing daylight. Lead your life with a blazing urgency and harness every moment.

Imagine for a moment a beggar who had been sitting on the side of the road for more than thirty years. One day a stranger walked by. "Spare some change?" mumbled the beggar, mechanically holding out his tattered baseball cap. "I have nothing to give you," said the stranger. Then he asked, "What are you sitting on?" "Nothing," replied the beggar. "Just an old box. I've been sitting on it for as long as I can remember." "You never looked inside?" asked the stranger. "No, what's the point?" "Look inside," insisted the stranger. The beggar managed to pry open the lid. With astonishment, disbelief, and elation, he saw that the box was filled with gold.

Abraham Maslow, the noted psychologist, called these moments "peak experiences." We can experience them not only once or twice a year but every day and every moment—if we put in the effort. Seize meditative moments and your dreams will come true. You'll stay true to your deepest values. Harness every day for spiritual recalibration and examination. Evaluate your life through the prism of your vision for who you want to be. Discover the opportunities both planned and unplanned to optimize every breath for renewal and reverse engineering your life!

Every day possesses the potential for growth and character development. Yet we all too often miss the latent opportunities. Ritualizing sacred space and a daily discipline for self-reflection provides the key to seizing your meditative moments.

Strategies

Daily Wake-Up Call: Your Brush with Death and Renewed Life

Do you walk in the dark or in the light? Do you chase daylight or meander in the darkness? In his epic novel *A Soldier of the Great War*, Mark Helprin expresses a pervasive frustration of modern man:

"When you walk through the city in the morning, what do you think about?" Alessandro asked his father.

"Many things."

"Do you think of the city itself?"

"No. I used to, but I've had a profession for a number of years, and it has mastered me. A profession is like a great snake that wraps itself around you. Once you are enwrapped, you are in a slow fight for the rest of your life, and the lightness of youth leaves you. You don't have time, for example, to think about the city even as you are walking through it."[4]

Helprin's lament is not only for the time that we invest in our careers. He's concerned, primarily, about the way our professions, and the anxieties and stress that accompany them, come to dominate our thoughts. When our thoughts are preoccupied by to-do lists that are never completed, we no longer notice the sights and sounds that surround us. We lose sight of our purpose and succumb to the ritual and routine of everyday life. We become tired and not inspired by our calling.

How do we remain alert? How do we savor the privilege of life?

One of the greatest philanthropists of the nineteenth century, Baron Rothschild was known not only for his riches but for his piety as well, not just in regard to his world-renowned charity and kindness but for his fear of God and strict adherence to his faith. He was a magnate who always stood ready to serve others. He alone stood ready to tend to his guest's needs and made sure that the stay at his home would be a most pleasant one.

One evening after his business affairs were complete, the baron knocked on the door of the guestroom and invited his guest to take a stroll in the expansive gardens surrounding his mansion. Along the scented paths, decorated with flowers and fruit trees, guest and host engaged in conversation. They passed by a small, well-maintained cottage on the outskirts of the garden. "What is this cottage for?" inquired the guest.

"It's my private office," the baron replied vaguely.

"Didn't you already show me a different room in your home that you said was your office?"

The baron thought for a moment and then looked around to make sure no one was within earshot. "Since you ask," he said in a whisper, "I'll reveal to you the secret of my 'other' office, the contents of which even my closest family members are not aware. Besides me, no one has ever stepped into this office."

The baron withdrew a key from his coat pocket and unlocked the cottage's door. Inside he lit a lamp, and his guest immediately froze in his spot. The cottage consisted of one windowless, completely bare room, save for a coffin that stood in the center of its floor. Inside the coffin were shrouds and a book about the laws of mourning.

Without waiting for the obvious question, the baron explained. "Every day, in the middle of my numerous business dealings, I quietly take a break and come to my 'office.' After locking the door behind me, I don the shrouds and lie inside the coffin. For about half an hour, I read the final confession and the prayers one says upon one's death-bed. This activity is vital to me. It ensures that I never, God forbid, become arrogant and start to believe I am invincible. Every day I must deal with great wealth flowing through my hands and 'rub shoulders' with numerous wealthy and famous contacts from all over the world. It would be all too easy for me to start believing that these are all my accomplishments, that my name and fame will live on forever. So, you see, I need this little reminder of the frailty of my existence and my total dependence on God."[5]

> *"Meditation on inevitable death should be performed daily. Every day one should meditate on being carried away by surging waves, falling from thousand-foot cliffs, dying of disease."*
>
> —Yamamoto Tsunetomo, samurai warrior

> *Rabbi Eliezer would say: "Repent one day before your death." He asked his disciples, "Does a man know on which day he will die?" He said to them, "So being the case, he should repent today, for perhaps tomorrow he will die; hence, all his days are passed in a state of repentance."*
>
> —Talmud Sabbath 153a

Tool Box

❶ **Study Mussar** (a Jewish cultural, ethical, and educational course of study) for fifteen minutes every day or another spiritual discipline. Make the heart feel what the intellect understands. For resources, visit *www.rabbidanielcohen.com*.

❷ **Mediate on psalms, poems, or prayers on the fragility of life** (e.g., Psalm 144):

> *Lord, what are human beings that you care for them,*
> *mere mortals that you think of them?*
> *They are like a breath;*
> *their days are like a fleeting shadow.*

❸ **Ritualize your mortality awakening.** Meditate on it daily. Here are some ideas: prayer, reading a journal or e-mails written when ill, a memento from the hospital, or whatever serves as a personal reminder of your humanity.

Sacred Scheduling

Life gets in the way. How many times have we said that we just didn't have the time for what was important in our lives? However, we possess the freedom to choose how we use our time. The challenge is developing the discipline to craft our own schedule and not be at the whim of others.

People ask me how I have time to write a book. I answer that I try not to waste time. How can I kill time? I believe that we're all endowed with the gift of life, days, hours, and minutes. Instead of being like a pinball moving from place to place and keeping busy, take time to decide how *you* want to spend your time. Make sure that at least an hour a day is spent cultivating your dreams, personal health, and spiritual life.

One of the tools I've found most helpful is based on the "Pareto principle," otherwise known as the 80/20 rule. It's named after the Italian economist Vilfredo Pareto. Examples of the principle include: 20 percent of our time produces 80 percent of our results; 20 percent of the presentation produces 80 percent of the impact. The concept affirms that 20 percent of our priorities will yield 80 percent of our results. If we focus on too much, we accomplish very little. As a headline in a recent article in *Success* magazine read, "Accomplish More by Doing Less" the key to achievement is not working harder but finding ways to do less and think more, be less busy and more productive.

Tool Box

Begin using the Pareto principle to obtain more fulfillment and balance in your life. Here's how Pareto works. Tasks are divided into four categories of priorities.

❶ **High importance/high urgency:** highest priority.

❷ **High importance/low urgency:** Set deadlines for completion and work on them in your daily routine. This is the place for seizing your meditative moments. Carve out time every day for mediation, growth, study, and health. Don't wait until they're urgent, such as when your life is on the line.

❸ **Low importance/high urgency:** Get done without much
personal involvement and, if possible, delegate.

❹ **Low importance/low urgency:** Busy work. Carve out time
once a week for a minimal amount of time. Perhaps you
don't need to do it at all.

Spending time defining the true priorities of responsibilities in
your life ensures that you'll spend 80 percent of your time on
the investments that yield the greatest dividends in your life.
To help you, answer these questions:

❶ Which activities are required of you every day?

❷ Which activities reflect your life aspirations?

❸ Which practices enable you to pause, reflect, and
reinvigorate your life mission?

❹ At the end of the day, what do you miss most if you haven't
found the time to do it?

Focus on these goals daily, weekly, and monthly. Every couple
of days, I answer these questions and fill out a Pareto form,
which forces me to stay focused on my long-term goals.
Also, keep the following tips in mind:

❶ **Just say no:** This is critical to creating space for what is
truly important. One yes is also a no to something else.
Time is limited. Use it wisely.

❷ **Study daily:** Choose a book, sacred text, or another source
of wisdom for reflection. Digest it and process how the
ideas apply to your life. This practice is crucial for

enriching your knowledge and spirit and, most important, for creating an objective barometer for your actions. The wisdom may move you outside your comfort zone, fostering personal growth.

❸ **Mentor:** Who do you turn to for advice? Who offers you wisdom and counsel? We all need support. Schedule a minimum of a monthly conversation with a mentor.

For a sample Pareto guide for daily prioritizing, visit *www.rabbid anielcohen.com*. Time is in your hands. Sanctify it and make your scheduling sacred.

The Power of Solitude

On the surface, solitude and loneliness seem similar, but they are, in fact, quite different. Loneliness is imposed upon us by others while solitude is chosen.

> *"All men's miseries derive from not being able to sit in a quiet room alone."*
>
> —Blaise Pascal

> *"Without great solitude no serious work is possible."*
>
> —Pablo Picasso

Throughout history, solitude served as the foundation for creativity, intellectual might, and spirituality. The leaders of the world's great religions—Moses, Muhammad, Jesus, and Buddha—all experienced revelations during periods of solitude. The poet James Lowell characterized solitude as "needful to the imagination." Beethoven, Kafka, and Newton are all examples of solitary geniuses.

One of my most vivid memories as an adult was traveling toward the south of Israel late at night with my family. We drove through the Makhtesh Ramon crater in the pitch-black. We stopped to get out of the car and were overwhelmed by the silence and the majesty of the stars above. They'd never appeared so bright and luminous. I sensed the spirit of David, who proclaimed, while gazing above, "The heavens declare the glory of God; the skies proclaim the work of his hands. Day after day they pour forth speech; night after night they reveal knowledge. They have no speech, they use no words; no sound is heard from them. Yet their voice goes out into all the earth, their words to the ends of the world" (Psalm 19).

Tool Box

❶ **Quiet your mind and disconnect from your mental drama.** Discover your internal power. Through solitude, you'll attune yourself to your inner voice.

❷ **Choose a quiet spot.** Be still. Ignore your demands. Turn off your phone and personal devices. Frequency is more important than duration. The length of time is not as important as consistency.

❸ **You can be still or move around.** Walk, run, sit, paint, fly-fish, hike, pray, meditate on a verse, think deeply.

❹ **Write in a journal.** Streams of consciousness reveal your innermost desires and serve as constant reminders of your life's deepest values.

Rabbi Abraham Kook remarked, "Every human being has a book inside of them waiting to be written." What is yours?

Meaningful Meditation

Meditation is not letting your mind wander but thinking in a controlled manner. It's directing your mind toward one topic. It's not easy and takes practice and training. This book isn't the place for a full exploration of this practice, but I encourage you to consider incorporating this discipline into your life. Praying consistently and with concentration provides one means of mediation. In particular, in the Jewish faith, praying in the morning, afternoon, and evening is intended as a three-pronged approach to realign your body and soul. The morning focus is gratitude, the afternoon is values and priorities, and the evening is faith.

Meditation offers many benefits. It quiets the mind and enables you to turn off all extraneous thoughts and "tune in to" the spiritual. In this sense, it's one of the most important techniques of mystics all over the world. Through studying meditation, we can see our own shortcomings and overcome them. We can learn to see the entire universe in a grain of sand. A person can meditate on a verse, a poem, nature, or even an object. In fact, meditation has been shown to lower stress. A recent study from Carnegie Mellon University, published in *Biological Psychiatry*, found that mindfulness meditation reduces inflammatory health biomarkers that have been linked to cancer, Alzheimer's, and autoimmune diseases.[6]

Tool Box

In many faith traditions, a flame carries spiritual significance. It symbolizes the soul pushing higher, the power of warmth, or community or passion for an ideal. Light a candle, dim the lights, and meditate on the flame. Try the following meditation. Use your answers as an opportunity to reorient your priorities and stay in tune with your best self.

❶ What do I ultimately want out of life?

❷ What gives my life meaning?

❸ What is the meaning of life in general?

❹ If I had to live my life over again, what would I do with it?

❺ What ideals, if any, would I be willing to die for?

❻ What would bring me more happiness than anything in the world?

*"The higher goal of spiritual living
is not to amass a wealth of information,
but to face sacred moments. Spiritual life begins
to decay when we fail to sense the grandeur of
what is eternal in time. . . . The Bible is more
concerned with time than with space.
It is more a record of sacred events
than sacred places."*

—Abraham Joshua Heschel

Rest or Renewal: The Sacred Sabbath

Growing up I never fully appreciated the beauty of the Sabbath. As my responsibilities have increased professionally and personally, I now realize that the Sabbath is my saving grace and the wind beneath my wings. The Sabbath transcends all faiths. We all need a sacred day for rejuvenation. One of my close friends is Pastor Greg Doll, and I share here his insights on the Sabbath for this important strategy for seizing our meditative moments.[7]

In the summer of 2012 my family and I were given the incredible gift of a three-month sabbatical. I returned from our time away feeling like an entirely different human being. I fumbled for a while to find a word that adequately described how I felt. I finally landed on one that worked—resurrected. I felt totally alive again, like a human phoenix—completely renewed from the inside out. We spent part of our time out West in Montana, Wyoming, and Colorado, fly-fishing some of the legendary Western streams. . . .

One of the toughest lessons in casting [while fly-fishing] is to allow the rod to do the work, to find the rhythm. One of the toughest lessons in the Christian life is to allow God to do his work of renewal in us, to find the spiritual rhythm.

My favorite line in the book, *A River Runs Through It* is when the author Norman MacLean says about his father the Presbyterian minister, "As for my father, I never knew whether he believed God was a mathematician but he certainly believed God could count and that only by picking up God's rhythms were we able to regain power and beauty [in our lives]."

Picking up God's rhythms is what restores our interior life, making it robust and vibrant—that's the power. The beauty is the ability to see all the wonder around us with a heart of thanksgiving. That's what happens when we slow down and allow the Holy Spirit to serve as our tour guide. "Only by picking up God's rhythms were we able to regain power and beauty [in our lives]."

One of the most surprising lessons I learned from the sabbatical is this: there is a big difference between rest and renewal. You can have weeks of rest with no work responsibilities, stay in places of extreme beauty and luxury and still feel ill at ease and restless and stressed.

In fact, I will go a bit farther and say that beautiful places, romantic places, quiet places, natural places can offer our bodies and minds wonderful rest but they can also be infuriating for their inability to deliver our souls into a place of rest.

I think that is the way God designed it. The natural world can only take us so far. Vacations can only take us so far. Only God can renew our souls. Each week God offers us the incredibly generous and loving gift of a mini-sabbatical to help renew our lives in the form of the Sabbath. The Sabbath was intended to be a weekly reminder that we are destined for joy, peace, freedom, rest, and abundance.

We are to construct a sanctuary in time where God can come and dwell. The One who renews us.

Listen to the way the rabbis described the Sabbath: "The seventh day is an exodus from tension . . . in the tempestuous ocean of time and toil there are islands of stillness where man may enter a harbor and reclaim his dignity. The island is the seventh day . . . It is a day of praise to God, not petitions. Fasting, mourning, demonstrations of grief are forbidden. It is a sin to be sad on the Sabbath day. This principle of Sabbath even applies to the animals and the fields. All of creation rests. *Six days you shall do all your labor and your work.* This is God's rhythm. Is it possible for a human being to do all his work in six days? The answer is: Does not our work always remain incomplete? Rest on the Sabbath as if all your work were done. Rest even from the thought of labor."

And so each week becomes a pilgrimage to the seventh day and the longing for the Sabbath each week becomes a form of longing for the eternal Sabbath.

Jesus said, "The Sabbath was made for you." It was a gift for you.

God's rhythm is six days of work and one day of rest.

The Sabbath begins at sundown. At that point everything stops. Because God says it is time to stop, not because our work is done. If we wait until our work is done, we will never stop. So God establishes the time. And so we are liberated from the need to be finished with our work.

It is really important to remember that the Sabbath is not just about slowing down and resting from our labors but also about hallowing time. We hallow it by setting it apart unto God. We do so by making it different from all the other days of the week.

How do we do it? A few brief thoughts:

1. Remember that the Sabbath is a gift from God who knows what we need. Commit to it. Don't miss out on it. Don't miss the blessing.
2. Do everything to make it different than the other days of the week. Try to avoid any form of work. Not because it is forbidden but to give yourself a break from work and to allow yourself to rest.
3. Allow yourself to rest in whatever form that takes for you.
4. Do what renews you. The Sabbath is not about prohibition but about freedom. Go out on your boat, tend your garden, play golf, go fishing, strum your guitar, etc.
5. Connect with Creation, with family, and with God. Do your best to make all those connections because God uses those connections

to renew us. Take a walk outside, share a meal with family and friends, worship, pray, study God's Word.

6. Avoid the things you do all week. For some it may mean not checking e-mail. Not searching the Internet. Not answering the telephone. Make the day altogether different from the other days of the week. Whatever that looks like for you.

> *"If you keep your feet from breaking*
> *the Sabbath and from doing as you please*
> *on my holy day, if you call the Sabbath a delight*
> *and the Lord's holy day honorable, and*
> *if you honor it by not going your own way*
> *and not doing as you please or speaking idle words,*
> *then you will find your joy in the Lord, and*
> *I will cause you to ride in triumph on the*
> *heights of the land and to feast on the inheritance*
> *of your father Jacob.' For the mouth*
> *of the Lord has spoken."*
>
> —(Isaiah 58:13–14)

May we discover the abundant, soul-satisfying, renewing life that leads us up to heights by receiving God's generous gift to us, the gift of the Sabbath—the gift of rest and abundant life.

Accounting of the Soul

We take an accounting of the body but why not the soul? The single most important practice to seize your meditative moments is a daily regimen of accounting for your spiritual life. In Jewish theology, the Hebrew term is "Cheshbon HaNefesh." It's a concept that spans the faith traditions. As Socrates stated, "The unexamined life is not worth living." Buy a journal and begin the process of daily reviewing your activities. Every day is a gift. Have you used it wisely?

Benjamin Franklin was one of the first people to recognize that recording your behavior helps you to change it. In fact, he turned self-development into a science by observing, monitoring, and measuring his behavior. In his autobiography, he identified thirteen virtues he would strive to live by: temperance, silence, order, resolution, frugality, industry, sincerity, justice, moderation, cleanliness, tranquillity, chastity, and humility.[8]

Tool Box

Every night before going to bed, look back at that day's events and evaluate where you profited or lost. Then make a plan so the next day will be more productive.

Ask yourself:

- What have I accomplished today?
- Did I accomplish what I intended?
- How am I going to improve for tomorrow?
- What are my strengths and weaknesses?
- What's my profit? What's my loss?
- How far have I come in my long-term goals?
- What's holding me back from growing?

Read over your list of mistakes and remind yourself, "This is the enemy." It might be laziness, or envy, or bad temper. Track down your own Achilles' heel, and concentrate on that. If you review your list daily and get angry at your own stupidities, then that anger will give you the power to make changes. An accounting of the soul reflects the importance of constant character development. There are many outstanding works to serve as guides. Some suggestions are *Meditations* by Marcus Aurelius, *The Ways of the Righteous* (written anonymously), or *The Path of the Just* by Rabbi Moshe Hayyim Luzzatto.

At the age of seventy-nine Benjamin Franklin wrote in his autobiography that he never did achieve his goal of attaining perfection. However, he did achieve the following: "Tho' I never arrived at the perfection I had been so ambitious of obtaining, but fell far short of it, yet I was, by the endeavor, a better and a happier man than I otherwise should have been if I had not attempted it."[9]

> *"For the wise have always known that no one*
> *can make much of his life until self-searching has*
> *become a regular habit, until he is able to admit and*
> *accept what he finds, and until he patiently and*
> *persistently tries to correct what is wrong."*
>
> —Bill Wilson

Celebrity Stirrings:
David Harris and Governor Dannel Malloy

> *"The mind's so far from the heart, they think*
> *and act as strangers."*
>
> —Michael Shapiro, *Return Home*

David Harris, executive director of the American Jewish Committee (AJC), one of the oldest Jewish advocacy organizations in the United States, shares what he does to seize meditative moments:

Opportunities abound to seize meditative moments and stay true to who we are and who we want to be in life. Primarily, in my case, morning and night, and it's seven days a week in my case. By morning and night, I mean that every morning I do roughly an hour of exercise, which until a few months ago when I had knee surgery, was a run. I don't speak to an Orthodox rabbi, but I run seven days a week.

I've been running since I was twenty, and before that I was playing team sports and things, and my run is always very much a spiritual period for me, in which I tend to review the day ahead, and I've always posed the challenge, especially since I've been working in this job, and also in previous jobs, of trying to come up with a new idea each and every day. It can be a big idea, it can be a small idea. It also allows me to inventory my relations with people, ideas for work—that's part of my spiritual experience every morning.

Every evening, I try, sometimes in that very brief moment between going to bed and falling asleep . . . especially after a long day, I try to inventory the day in terms not just of, gee, what did I do? Or did I not do? But did anything I did today have any particular meaning or impact that went beyond the moment. That's the kind of mental discipline that I've tried to have over many, many, many years, as again, I very much believe in the notion of the examined life. On the eve of Easter . . . here's a nice Jewish boy, I know that this is a sacred holiday for Christians . . . the most sacred holiday of the year for Christians, are there Christian employees at AJC, sung and unsung, to whom I should be dropping a note, wishing them a happy Easter? Are there people who are sick or facing illness at

AJC that I should be sending a brief note to, "How are you?"; just checking in. I go through this each and every day, seven days a week, 365 days a year, no matter where I am.

The governor of Connecticut, Dannel Patrick "Dan" Malloy, shares his thoughts on his own personal system of seizing meditative moments:

> My system is instant reflection. When there's a moment, I'm reflective. I reflect on the things that I'm doing short-term, long-term, what I've done in the past. I had to respond on December 14 in Newtown and help the community deal with that situation. It evolved over a few hours of time. Within those few hours, there were absolutely periods of reflection on what I was going to do, and how I reached decisions were being reflected upon on an ongoing basis in real time because when responding to a crisis, you can't say, "Hey, I need to take a timeout. I have to have the ability to take a deep breath and step back immediately."

CHAPTER 5

━━

Principle No. 4:
Create Memories

I'm now forty-nine years old. Time moves ever faster. I feel and I imagine that many of us know how quickly one day passes into the next, month into month and year into year. Looking back, I find it hard to believe that we have daughters who are almost out of school and ready to enter the workforce. Our daughters range from ages thirteen to twenty-four. It seems like just yesterday that I met Diane on our first date in New York City, and I experienced intuitive feelings of elation after I said good-bye, knowing she was someone truly special. I kid my daughters that when we got married more than twenty-five years ago, we knew we'd have six daughters. Who could've imagined! I thank God for our blessings!

Yet, as we celebrated our youngest daughter Shalhevet's Bat Mitzvah this past year, the last one of our girls to mark the transition into

Jewish adulthood, I experienced a sensation unlike for any of our other daughters. As the weekend approached, I felt a sense of loss. This would be the final Bat Mitzvah celebration for our family as parents. It was hard to believe. I began to mourn the memory of a Bat Mitzvah before it had even happened. Slowly, I realized that though it was human nature to lament the fragility of life and the passage of time, this was not a time to mourn but to celebrate. We did everything possible to make the weekend as full, memorable, and meaningful as possible. My father offered me his weekly blessings on Friday, an hour before the celebration commenced: "Enjoy the simcha, enjoy the celebration!" Thank God, we did!

In a moment that I wanted to last forever, I offered the following words at the conclusion of my charge to Shalhevet: "There is a tradition in Jewish weddings for a special dance on the occasion of the last wedding of one's children. Well, today we celebrate our last daughter's Bat Mitzvah. Let's dance! In the words of King David, 'This is the day God has made, let us rejoice and be glad in it.'" I began to sing, and the congregation erupted in song and dance, and even lifted me up on a chair and carried me about. Our souls were singing and Shalhevet's Bat Mitzvah was unforgettable!

I share this story at the outset of the chapter on creating memories because it speaks to our humanity, and the challenges and opportunities it affords. Life does flash by. There are moments when we sense, ever so painfully, our life as a highlight film. Yet we can slow down time and enrich every experience with significance and depth when we forge eternally enriching memories. Do not mourn the passage of time but celebrate the inherent possibilities in the gift of every moment.

How do we stay true to the principle of creating memories? Which experiences become memorable and which ones fade into the recesses of time? Which experiences drift away and which ones pulsate forever? Let's explore this principle together.

As a rabbi officiating at hundreds of funerals, I'm struck by the memories children share in tribute to their parents. It's impossible to summarize a life in twenty minutes, but what memories endure? The words of Dr. Seuss ring true: "Sometimes you will never know the value of a moment until it becomes a memory."

I'll never forget driving with my parents to find a scenic spot overlooking the fireworks celebration at Lenox Mall in Atlanta. We sat atop the hood of our car in the heat, waiting for the spectacle in the sky. Ironically, the most impactful memory wasn't the actual fireworks but the ride in the car with the family in tow and the joyous expectation as we rode together on the hilly roads and watched the darkening skies.

I remember this moment so vividly for at least two reasons. It was a moment we experienced together as a family, and a moment shared is one of the hallmarks of an enduring memory. But, more important, the experience reveals a fundamental truth: *In life, the destination is not nearly as important as the journey*. We got into the car for a family outing to watch the fireworks, which ironically yielded a temporary burst of light, but the lasting lights were generated on the ride and by spending time together.

The cost of creating a memory is minimal. It's not about how much money is spent, whether on a gift or a vacation, but on the attention, focus, and time we give one another. The benefits are priceless.

Listen closely to a secret I'm about to share. It will transform the way you live and the way you'll be remembered: *We don't remember days, we remember moments*. Think back on the lives of the people close to you. What stands out? Usually it's an experience we shared with them or a moment in time. The days become a blur, but the best memories are when it seems like time stands still and we share an experience we'll never forget.

Do we appreciate the impact of memories we create in the hearts and minds of family and friends? One of the happiest moments of my life was walking to synagogue with my father in the pouring rain. Although we were soaked, my spirit soared. There was no place I'd rather be at that moment than holding my father's hand on the way to synagogue. The moment embodied the love and respect of a father and the shared, timeless value of the sanctity of the Sabbath. Little did my father know the impact of these timeless moments together.

In a dramatic and poignant way, this idea further resonated within me at a funeral this past year. I encouraged one of the daughters to share memories of her mother. Her relationship with her mother had been challenging, yet I urged her to take the opportunity to thank her mother and reflect briefly on her legacy. She introduced her remarks by stating that over the span of fifty years with her mother, two memories stood out. This is one of them that she shared: "I'll never forget when I was eight years old. I was fast asleep. My mother came into my room around midnight. It was snowing outside and she woke me. I was startled and wondered why she had disturbed my sleep. I'll never forget what she said that night. She told me she wanted me to get dressed so we could go play together in the fresh snow outside." She had fifty years of life with her mother, but what she remembered was a spontaneous expression of love when she was a child decades earlier.

When do a child's formative years begin? Someone once posed this question to Rabbi Samson Raphael Hirsch while accompanied by their three-year-old child, and he responded, "You missed the best three years of his life!"

Judaism teaches that from birth we create impressions on our children that shape their futures. The Talmud debates the youngest age appropriate for taking one's child on a pilgrimage to Jerusalem for the festivals. The sages conclude that whether the child can walk or be carried on our shoulders, toddlers are old enough to imbibe the spiritual sounds and sights of a rendezvous with God and community.

Think about it for a moment. What will a small child we're carrying on our shoulders remember? Even if they can just hold our hands and walk with us, what impression will endure? Herein lies a fundamental truth to creating memories: *People may not remember what we say, but they'll remember how we make them feel.*

Thinking back on my own life and my career in the rabbinate, I trace some of my spiritual stirrings to an experience I had as a young child in the 1970s. I don't remember a word my father uttered, but I'll never forget the experience. I can remember holding my father's hand as I walked down a dark alley in Atlanta. It was at the height of the Soviet Jewry movement, and rallies fighting for religious freedom and the right of the Jews to leave the former Soviet Union were being held in cities across the country. Many of the refuseniks were incarcerated for practicing their faith. They lived thousands of miles from my home. Their plight was not mine. Yet my father bringing me to this rally and the feeling of seeing Jews holding flags, dancing, and singing "Am Yisrael Chai" (The Jewish nation will live) etched a memory onto my soul forever.

I don't remember words from the rally, but the feeling lives on. Joining my father, holding his hand, this mission still pulsates within me, drives me, and guides me more than forty years later. I'd venture to say that my father didn't know the impression these few minutes would make on my life, but they affirm the power of memories to create a legacy. Holding my father's hand as a young child on a holy mission altered my life and my children's lives forever.

Ironically, many years later, I reminded my father of the indelible impression he had made on me when another special impact opportunity arose. My father and stepmother were moving to Israel, and we wanted to bring our girls to the airport so they could witness this historic moment for our family.

My father told me that he would rather I not spend three hours driving but use the time to study Torah. I responded to him that going to the airport was not for us but for our children. Diane and I wanted our children to see their grandparents and other families who chose to immigrate and establish new homes in Israel. My father remarked, "Aha, you are right," as he knew the impact that such trips had on me as a child.

In every moment we are forging memories for the future.

What memories are we creating today that will last in our lifetimes and beyond?

> **"To live in the hearts we leave**
> **behind is not to die."**
>
> —Thomas Campbell, Scottish poet

A selection from the Ethics of the Fathers reminds every person, "Know that God is above you and all of your deeds are recorded for posterity." Every act that we do reverberates in time and endures.

How do we create such moments? The answer lies in ensuring that we're living in these moments. As the popular quote says, "Life is not measured by the breaths you take but by the moments that take your breath away."

Time does go by quickly, but if we pause and reflect on the second we're experiencing and sense the opportunity within—to be present with a spouse, a friend, or a child, to lend a hand, make a blessing, study one insight—the fleeting moment can be eternalized. What will happen is that not only will these memories be etched into our hearts but our lives will now be much more meaningful. With this perspective, we'll be able to transform our lives and those around us . . . one step at a time.

As we continue through this chapter of creating memories, you'll be awakened to the innate potential we all possess to live forever in the hearts and minds of those whom we encounter. Like one candle, your soul can light many eternal flames. You will learn:

- How to slow down time as the secret to creating memories.
- Strategies to enrich relationships and forge meaningful connections with people.
- How to invest in moments and not monuments.
- The power of a word, a walk, and a touch.
- How to captivate, to educate.

Seize opportunities to create memories that reflect your dreams and values, and in the words of Bob Dylan, "If you want to keep your memories, you first have to live them."

Foundations

How do we want to be remembered? "What will they say about you when you're gone?" is a question that taps into an innate quest we possess for immortality and making a difference in the world. We struggle to transcend the finite boundaries of time.

Throughout the history of humanity, humans have striven to become immortal. From Ponce de León's quest for the fountain of youth to the building of monuments, we strive to outlast our mortality and defeat death. This isn't because we know we can physically transcend the limits of time but rather because programmed into our DNA is a desire to be remembered, to lead a life of significance. We all want to know that we made some everlasting contribution to the world.

"One lives in the hope of becoming a memory."

—Antonio Porchia, Argentinian poet

Look at the world around you. The highways and byways, buildings, and monuments are named after people. There's value to investing one's resources in the establishment of a program or institution to perpetuate a legacy. When we walk into a hospital, for instance, we notice the wall of donors. We're grateful for people's generosity, yet when we explore the principle of creating memories, we're focusing on a more universal dimension to legacy.

In truth, testaments of brick and mortar are not the ones that are ultimately eternal. The sonnet "Ozymandias" by Percy Bysshe Shelley expresses this idea forcefully. The poem speaks of a ruler of the ancient world, a master of other countries, and the peoples who immortalize his kingdom through the establishment of a sphinx. The tomb tells a very different story. It is "shattered" and surrounded by a desert "boundless and bare." Despite his enormous wealth and notoriety, Ozymandias becomes a footnote in history. The poem conveys a fundamental truth of leading a life of legacy. The things we do outlast our mortality. *We live on, not in the monuments we create but in the hearts and minds of those we touch.* The most enduring memories are not forged through a building but through people. An emotional exchange between two souls and two people endures forever.

Think back for a moment of the experiences you'll never forget, not ones that simply left you feeling good but ones that resonate deeply within you to this day. What memories stay with you? When we seek to reverse engineer our lives, we're living in a way that will enrich the here and now, deepen relationships, and plant the seeds for immortality. This book, and the principle of creating memories in particular, forge the essence of leading a meaningful life.

If we allow our lives to fly by without full consciousness of the moment we're experiencing, we'll never realize our full potential, and we'll sense emptiness inside. The feeling of joy and fulfillment emerges not only from maximizing every day as living inspired but in knowing that we shared our lives with others. When we love, when we intertwine our souls with another, we create an eternal bond. Our attempt to create memories is the strategy to leading a life of transcendence.

What Is the Anatomy of a Memory That Endures?

An everlasting memory is forged when we establish a connection between another person, a soul. A memory cannot be bought but must be shared. The best gifts in the world are not the material objects one can buy from the store but the memories we make with the people we love.

Think back on your life and your enduring memories. I'm sure so many fill your mind. Choose one from when you were a child. I remember the time on the Sabbath when we'd recite grace after meals. We'd sing the prayers out loud. As we approached the final paragraph, the rhythm of the tune would speed up, and I remember running to my father's lap, where he bounced me up and down until, right at the very end, I slid to the floor.

This idea hit home during the celebration of Hanukkah in our family, a scene that is not uncommon across all faith traditions. One evening my daughters arranged to share gifts in our version of the Secret Santa. We call it the Mystery Maccabee. The excitement surrounding the opening of gifts and the genuine appreciation of the care taken in getting just the right one was more memorable than the value and utility of the gift itself. We remember the joy and the love. Minutes before, we lit candles and paused to meditate on the moment, to truly appreciate what we were experiencing.

Herein lies an important reality. If we're too focused on creating the memory, we won't be in the moment. It's like the person who records his child's play and fiddles with the camera to get just the right angle, all while missing the actual performance and reveling in the moment.

To create memories, we can't forget to be present with the people who are right in front of our eyes.

I learned this lesson when I missed seeing the gorilla. While at a training program at the Kellogg School of Management at Northwestern University, my colleagues and I were asked to watch a video clip of kids passing a basketball, and we were asked to count the number of passes. At the conclusion of the scene, we were asked two questions: (1) How many passes? and (2) Did you see the gorilla? Almost to a T, we counted the same number of passes. However, only half of us saw the gorilla in costume, waving its arms as it walked through the passing basketballs. When watching the video a second time, it was so obvious. How could we have missed it?

We learned then that we were participants in an experiment first conducted at Harvard University entitled "Gorillas in Our Midst" and later described in the book *The Invisible Gorilla: How Our Intuitions Deceive Us* by Christopher Chabris and Daniel Simons. The study documented the pervasive influence of the illusion of attention. We were told to count the basketball passes, so we did, but we missed the gorilla thumping its chest right in front of our eyes. *We think we're seeing the world as it is, but we're really missing so much.*

Enjoy life while you're living it. Be open for anything at any time. In the words of Oscar Wilde, "To live is the rarest thing in the world. Most people exist, that is all."

Think about it for a moment. How do relationships break down? The number one key ingredient to a lasting bond between spouses, parents, and children is time together. We can be in the same room or the same house, but are we truly with one another? There may be little communication and connection. Technology intrudes on our lives like nothing has before. Work comes home with us, and the dividing lines of personal and business time are blurred. We may be more engaged with someone online than we are with the person sitting across the table from us. We may be under the illusion that we're paying attention to our children or a friend, but are we truly present and in the moment? When we live fully present with those we love, we can transform even the most mundane experiences into eternal ones.

When we experience life this way, we discover the deepest joys. It's a happiness that emerges from soul sensations. Our souls want to love and be loved, and when we quench this inner desire, we feel so alive! Reverse engineering your life speaks to the possibility we possess to forge a memory all the time.

How do we answer the phone? Do we lose our temper or stay patient in the presence of our children or friends? When someone speaks to us, are we listening or merely giving the impression that we're present when our minds are actually elsewhere?

In truth, we're creating memories all the time. This idea is both haunting and inspiring. I'm often taken aback when someone says they remember a conversation I had with them or a kind gesture I made of which I have no recollection. We'll never know what action we do or words we say that will be remembered. Harness every word and moment, and act for eternity.

John Donne wrote, "No man is an island." We're all onstage and interconnected to one another. What we do, what we say, and how we behave are not private but public and impact our families and community. Our actions may not be posted on the front page of the newspaper or in the headlines on social media, but they endure nonetheless. It may be a comment we might forget, but for another, it's unforgettable.

What memories did your parents forge in your consciousness that shaped who you are today? In speaking with Tamir Goodman, known as the Jewish Jordan for his commitment to observe the Sabbath and maintain his religious principles while playing NCAA Division One basketball, I gained new insight into the power of memories created in small but significant ways. He shared the following: "When I was about eight years old, I hit the game-winning shot in a local recreational league. I was just so excited because basketball meant everything to me. I was pumping my arms in the air as if I was the greatest player. When I got back in the car, my father told me words I will never forget. 'I'm very proud of you; you played well, you hit the game-winning shot, but a Jewish person never reacts like that.' Never react as if your talents are coming because of your own hard work. You need to remember that your talent and basketball is a gift."

When I asked him the source of his strength to follow his faith and not the allure of the national stage of basketball, he shared, "I remember going into court with my father and seeing him wearing a kippah in court. All the Jewish lawyers there could see how proud he was of his faith. He always focused on what was important in life. He never put an emphasis on materialistic things. Things that were important to him were religion, his family, and helping others. He made everyone feel good. He was always there for us. No matter what was going on, no matter how busy, no matter what kind of case he was involved in, he had a big firm, but if we needed anything, he was there in a second. Those are the things that I'll always remember about him."

Tamir's father understood one of the most important dimensions of creating memories and instilling enduring values: To educate is not to capture but to captivate. Engaging the mind is not nearly as important as captivating the heart. Our children learn from what we do more than what we say.

What will your children or loved ones say about you?

I'm inspired by how words shared can motivate someone for a lifetime. Think for a moment about a piece of advice given to you that shaped who you are today. Maybe it was from a teacher, parent, or friend. Anne Curry, a well-known television personality and news journalist who has been a humanitarian reporter for more than thirty years, whom I interviewed, credits her father with her life's mission:

I remember when I was very young, maybe I was eight or nine, asking my father what I should be when I grew up. My father paused, and he said, "Anne, whatever you decide, do something that is of some service to somebody else. Then, and only then, will you know on your last day as you breathe your last breath that it mattered that you were here." Then, when I was ten and I asked, and when I was twelve, and thirteen, and fourteen, and whenever I asked him the question, the answer was always the same. The question and that motivation from him lasted all the way through the years until I lost him.

This idea that there isn't a lot of time and we have to live in this present manner, I think, has been a part of his lesson to me, essentially, almost my entire life. The idea is to live a life of service because you do want to matter. You do want people who love you, especially, to feel as though you contributed to their lives, and then you realize when you start to learn about the world that everyone is connected in ways that most of us don't realize fully. We're really all sisters and brothers and connected to each other. *You want in some manner to be of some service.* Now, there's a kind of ego in the idea that I want to feel good about myself when I have to face my last day, but there's also a kind of altruism as well. I think that the balance of that is important, that really the energy is about what good you can do in the time that you're here.

When choosing my career to be a journalist, to be someone who tells stories, who reaches out to places people don't know about and tries to make connections between those places and the people who are listening or reading what I create, what I'm trying to do is let people understand something that makes them better, deeper, and bigger. They know something about somebody else, and I think, ultimately, almost every story is really about us. It's really about our willingness or nonwillingness to accept the suffering of someone else. It's about our joy at seeing something fantastic, and it's a shared experience with other people, because we're all human beings, and we all love seeing something joyful. It's really about that. It's about connections, so this has been the biggest thing for me. The biggest lesson has been this lesson from my father and this idea that we are here for more than ourselves.

Anne's father, Bob Curry, died after a battle with cancer in the spring of 2012. In remembering him, she shared how his mantra of service in word and deed energizes her career and her life. Anne is known for her altruistic spirit as a journalist and human being. For instance, in the wake of the Sandy Hook school shootings in Newtown, Connecticut, she launched the initiative "26 Acts of Kindness" in memory of the twenty students and six teachers who were murdered. Her raison d'être stems from her father's words of wisdom decades earlier.

Think for a moment of the people who Anne impacts and the timeless resonance of a father's advice to his daughter. Think about your own children and grandchildren and the import of your words and deeds for them. What word can you share today that will resonate into the future? Sometimes even the simplest of acts as parents or grandparents may etch a mark on a child's soul forever and shape the trajectory of their life.

Imagine you're riding on a packed bus with your seated child. There are no more available spots, and at the next stop an elderly person gets on the bus. What do you say to your child? Do you wait to see if someone else makes room for the woman or do you immediately get up yourself and seize the opportunity to inspire generosity in your child? You're getting off the bus in a few stops, so maybe you just wait until then. Our decisions on that day may reverberate forever. What impression are we making on our children? For David Harris, one of the world leaders in global advocacy for human rights and ethnic understanding as executive director of the American Jewish Committee, his mother's decision on a bus stirs within him to this day.

When I was growing up, again, I remember very well being on the 104 bus, which was a Broadway bus, because I grew up on the West Side in Manhattan, as a young man. As soon as an elderly person came, my mother said, "Get up." Very nicely, very politely, but it wasn't a choice. "David, get up." "Mom, I'm tired. You know, I played basketball." "David, she's more tired than you are."

A blind person comes on to a bus or a train car. The easiest thing is to avert one's eyes because, I've got a seat; I'm tired; I've had a long day; my leg hurts, whatever. Look, there's someone younger than me sitting at that seat, he should be getting up, not me. There are all kinds of ways we can rationalize our own decision making, in a way that tries to create a zone of comfort.

But at the end of the day, when the blind person comes on the bus, or the elderly woman carrying a bag, it's not about the others on the bus, it's about me. If I choose to get up and give my seat, and a younger person says to me, "Well actually, sir, you should sit down because I should stand up," maybe I'll sit down because he stood up. But if he's not going to stand up, it's about me not him. The easiest thing for me is to go home and say to my spouse, "Can you imagine, I was on a bus and I was sitting on the bus, and an elderly person came. There were three young people . . . and they didn't get up! Shocking how young people are today!"

The scene on the bus is symbolic of the struggle we face every day to lead a life of significance. Wise Jewish sages taught that when a baby is born, its hands are clenched because, not knowing any better, it wants to grab everything, the whole world. But when old people die, their hands are open because they've learned the lesson that they can take nothing with them. Life is about moving from being self-centered to being other centered. It's about moving outside our comfort zone, even in the seemingly small decisions. Do I get up for another or do I remain seated? Do I extend a greeting or keep my head down? David Harris's mother instilled the value of opening his hands to help another. The memory on the bus shaped his life and, in turn, the thousands of people who he continues to touch.

Governor Dan Malloy credits his mother with cultivating his confidence and innate commitment to making the world a brighter place. He shared:

> I think about the way I was raised and the circumstances under which I was raised. I had severe learning disabilities and physical disabilities that I had to overcome to be successful. When I say overcome, I had to develop compensatory skills for the learning disabilities. The physical disabilities I did work through. My mother had a philosophy. It was not to worry about the things that I wasn't good at. It was to build on the things that I had strength in. From the skill set of being a good oral communicator and having really natural leadership skills, I think she really promoted that I might choose public service.
>
> She also did some other interesting things. My mother insisted on her children, particularly me, volunteering, visiting people in nursing homes for instance. Just go in and make their day brighter. She would actually drive me and say, "Get out of the car and go visit people and make their day brighter." I was raised to find a reward in public service, and the reward required that you did the right thing.

Chuck Leavell (who we met earlier as a member of the Allman Brothers Band and the Rolling Stones) reflected on the inspiration of his mother on his career in music:

> I was the youngest of three children: my sister, five years my elder, and my brother, fourteen years my elder. Oftentimes it was just the two

of us in the house with my father out working and my brother and sister in school when I was four, five, six years old. We spent a lot of time together. She was not a professional or a teacher but she played for family enjoyment. I used to love to listen to her play piano. I would say one of the greatest memories is the two of us being in the house and her playing and me listening and then her encouraging me to sit at the stool. Showing me some very simple things and encouraging me to play music. That's how I learned how to play. She was just a great inspiration.

A child's nature develops over time, a period in which the child is impressionable. Our role as adults can have a lasting impact on his or her personality. Noted English philosopher John Locke said that children are born as a "blank slate" (tabula rasa) and are morally neutral: "We are all like chameleons; we take our hue and the color of our character from those around us."

Never underestimate the impression we can make and the opportunities we can offer our youth. Their approach to life is in no small measure due to the spirit we implant in them. As Locke remarked, "Parents wonder why the streams are bitter, when we have poisoned the foundation." If your fountain is effervescent and positive, the streams will flow with strength and vitality for years to come. Create memories now and forever, and lead the life now for how you want to be remembered.

Creating Memories: Wheelchairs and the New York Public Library

When we reflect on the impact of what our children see us do and how the impression we make on them can truly reverberate throughout history, it's awe-inspiring! For anyone who has been to New York City and passed by the grand hall of the New York City Public Library, we sense the magnificence of the structure and, more important, the significance of this venue as an equalizer where everyone has the opportunity to learn and grow. One of the main benefactors, Steve Schwarzman of Blackstone, one of the world's leading investment firms, shared his inspiration for philanthropy with me:

> My father's father, Jacob Schwarzman, inspired me at a very young age to participate in charity. He would always save money and buy wheelchairs and buy other things. I guess it was either once a month or every two months, he'd have all these things wrapped up in our storage room and ship them to Israel. He was always giving away money and educating us all that this was an obligation. That's pretty odd. I never saw a wheelchair before. He was supporting charity and Israel. He sent them things, he gave them money, and he did other things. These were impactful moments as a five-year-old, six-year-old, and eight-year-old, seeing that type of behavior and getting lectures on the right thing to do.

How are you cultivating a sense of generosity in your children or grandchildren?

Tool Box

❶ Be a role model: Volunteer your time for a charity. Values are caught not taught. Be generous yourself. Your children will learn from you!

❷ Small acts count: Make it a habit to cultivate a routine of giving. Keep a charity box in your home. Take your small change from the day and put it in the box. Encourage others to do so as well.

❸ Open your home: Welcome guests. It's easy to host friends. Perhaps there is someone you know who's without family and would appreciate an invitation for a meal.

❹ Team effort: Invite your children to join you in your volunteer effort. Talk to them about the cause, teach them about its merits, and then get involved together!

❺ The gift of giving: When you give a money gift to your children or grandchildren, do so with the proviso of giving some of it to charity. Try giving money in threes: one third is for saving, one third is for giving, and one third is to use however the child likes.

Heart to Heart

> *"Share your knowledge.*
> *It is a way to achieve immortality."*
>
> —Dalai Lama XIV

We hope that our influence lingers long after we're gone. One way to assure this is to literally share our wisdom with another. I'd like to take the Dalai Lama's insight shared in the quote above a step further. Legacy is not simply created by the transfer of information. Words of impact, particularly ones that stick, are not simply given from a trove of knowledge, which may often emerge from the head and not the heart. The Talmud explains that what comes from our hearts goes into another person's heart. Whether friends, children, or students, we sense authenticity and are inspired by it.

When we think about the most influential teachers in our lives, they're the ones who not only conveyed information but did so with passion and love. Think about the most meaningful conversations you've had in your life. Which words stick with you over the years? Whether from a parent to a child, a friend to a friend, or even a heartfelt word to a stranger, *heartfelt words can penetrate another soul and transcend the limits of time.*

When I sit down with a family to prepare for the funeral of a parent, I always ask, "What words of wisdom did your mother or father share with you? What memories or mantras motivate you? What values did they embody that live in you?" It's true that values are caught more often that taught, but we shouldn't underestimate the value of explicit guidance to our children or grandchildren. Taking the time and crystallizing life wisdom for future generations will yield eternal dividends.

One of the most prominent philanthropists in the Jewish world shared the following memory with me, which inspires me and guides him as a father and grandfather:

I am very, very open and direct with our kids. It's not so easy to do that in this culture, right? My father had not an ounce of political correctness. Zero. We always knew exactly where he stood. We may not have liked it, but he always told us exactly what he thought, whether he thought that we would take to it, that we would absorb it, and that it would resonate with us. It was never charged with anger. Even as adults, here I was in my fifties, and my father would tell me exactly, "Look, you don't have to agree with me, but you need to know where I stand and how I think about this." He would not always, but very often criticize me for not being open enough and direct enough with my kids. He says, "You're coddling them. They have to know."

Right before my Bar Mitzvah, my father sat me down and talked to me about the obligation to give 10 percent of my income to charity. My grandfather had sat my father down before his Bar Mitzvah to tell him the same thing. My father said, "Whatever God blesses you with, you have to understand that you have to give 10 percent, and if one day you are successful and do very well in business or in your profession, you need to understand that if you look historically, all the wealthy families from the nineteenth century or early twentieth century in Germany and other parts of Europe, their fortunes have dwindled, with the exception of one: the Rothschilds. Why? Because they were meticulous, and to this day continue to be meticulous, about giving 10 percent. If you don't give maaser [tithe], you're not going to be able to keep your wealth."

At the time he said, "God willing, before your son becomes a Bar Mitzvah, you need to have the same conversation with him," and I did. He said, "How do we know that they gave maaser? Not from their tax returns. They kept meticulous records about what they gave to charities, from Mayer Amschel [Rothschild] all the way down to today. They kept very meticulous records of what they give."

We grew up in a very warm, cohesive community. My father was one of the leaders of the community and gave freely, not just with what he was able to give in terms of money but in terms of his time, effort, and work, and, besides that, just being very busy within the community. That was the most powerful example of all.

One of the foundations of reverse engineering our lives is having an awareness that our actions reflect on our past and will reverberate into the future long after we walk the earth. What we do matters. We are who we are because of previous generations who invested in us. What values embody the legacy of your family? What stories, mottos, and models do you embrace that will serve as guideposts for your children or grandchildren's future? As Warren Buffet shared, "Someone is sitting in the shade today because someone planted a tree a long time ago."

Tool Box

❶ **Family values:** Great companies possess a statement of values or a mission. What is yours? We plan for our children's financial future by establishing trusts, but even more important, we're instilling values. Craft a family declaration of values or a letter with wisdom. Make sure that you, too, are living up to it. One of the most famous letters of a parent to a child was written by Rabbi Moshe ben Nachman, also known as Nachmanides, to his son (for the text, see *http://www.magendavid.org/page.asp?ID=23*).

❷ **Family heirlooms:** Look around your house. Do you have an object that was passed down to you and reflects the legacy of your family? Share the story with your children and grandchildren. Create a new heirloom, perhaps a ritual item you use on special occasions, a photo montage, scrapbook, or meaningful item that symbolizes your aspirations.

❸ **Heart to heart:** Sit down with your loved one and share wisdom from your ancestors or your own experience. What's the most important advice you could give your child and/or grandchild? Share it from your heart.

❹ **Craft a family genealogy chart.** This process reveals stories, connections, and a sense of generational transcendence.

❺ **Write a memoir.** My father (he should live and be well) has written a few books, and he shared his purpose with me: "My teacher, Rabbi Lichtenstein, said that our role is to be a messenger for future generations, to leave a legacy for others. I think that is why I derive satisfaction from writing books. In truth, whatever I have written is for my children. The books may deal with Torah, with parenting, with film, but embedded in the pages are life lessons for my children. Read the books. Hear Abba's [Father's] voice reverberating into the future."

Love Letters: In Memory of My Mother

When we contemplate the power of creating memories, letter writing looms large. With the development of social media and the Internet, it's easier than ever to stay in touch with people. Whether a text, a tag, or Instagram, we can communicate instantaneously. Yet the ease of communication perhaps diminishes the depth of our message. I don't save e-mails generally, but a handwritten letter crafted with love and thought stays in my soul.

Two of the most important women in my life, my grandmother and mother, were avid letter writers. My grandmother, who immigrated to America as a young girl in the 1920s and remained forever grateful for the opportunities in America, gifted each of her grandchildren with a letter on the bicentennial of America. She handwrote a note reminding us of the freedom offered in the United States of America and the promise of "Lady Liberty," as she characterized the Statue of Liberty. We all cherish these letters and her aspirations for us embedded within. On the twenty-fifth anniversary of my mother's passing, I dreamed of her letters and the secret of her ever-presence in my life. Although time marches on, she feels close to me every day, and I sense her presence all the time.

When I was a child, my parents sent me and my siblings to a sleep-away camp in the Catskills. Almost every summer, we packed the car and my dad drove us from Atlanta to New York. Although I enjoyed camp for the most part, it was hard to be so far away from home, and I was homesick. I was only allowed one call home on visiting day. Letters were my only communication with my parents.

Last night, I dreamed of the joy in opening up a letter from my mother. She would write almost daily just telling me about her day. I can see her neat handwriting, the opening salutation of "Dear Dani," and the closing "Love, Ima." She would often add a smile. Those letters transcended space, and I felt her warmth and love hundreds of miles away. She knew I needed a hug, and she was there for me.

> *"All my life I have written letters—*
> *to our mother, our relatives, a wide circle of*
> *friends and acquaintances, to my husband, to you.*
> *Correspondence has always been as necessary*
> *to my happiness as a well-cooked dinner, and*
> *I've found it more sustaining for its generosity:*
> *an act of charity that returned*
> *to me a hundredfold."*
>
> —Delia Sherman, *The Porcelain Dove*

Tool Box

❶ **Offer words of encouragement to someone every day.**

❷ **On a birthday, anniversary, or milestone, write a letter** letting someone know how much you appreciate them and how much they mean to you.

❸ **On a sticky note, let someone know how much you love them.** Put it on a backpack, pillow, and desk, and make it consistent. One person, Jessie Hale, decided to let his wife know that he loves her for one hundred days—using sticky notes (*http://www.huffingtonpost.com/2014/02/14/ jesse-hale_n_4790250.html*).

Walking Together

I no longer have any living grandparents. My mother's mother passed away this year at the age of 101. We miss her greatly but feel eternally blessed for her love, wisdom, honesty, and zest for life. She'll always be a part of our lives. When I drive up the Henry Hudson Parkway and pass the exit for the Hebrew Home in Riverdale where she lived for the past eight years of her life, my heart skips a beat, as we'd often stop by for a visit. I mourn the fact that new members in our family will only know her through our memories of her. She was a life force who immigrated to America almost a hundred years ago with her family from Europe and planted the roots in our country for future generations. We're fortunate that she wrote a memoir many years ago that traces the arc and color of our family's history. Her soul looms large in my life, not because of the book she wrote but the time we shared. We spent many holidays together and enjoyed many visits at her home and ours in New York, Atlanta, and Florida. But what stands out most are the walks we took together.

Invariably, when we were in Florida, I'd walk around the golf course on Country Club Drive with her. Our topics would range from the mundane to the holy, plans for vacation, family life, and my career and life aspirations. Walking together created the sacred space to focus on each other and share our disappointments and dreams. The simplicity of a walk, side by side, without distractions, holding hands, evokes within us a return to self and who we want to be. I'm not surprised that some of my deepest memories of my grandparents emerge from these walks, for they create the foundation for shared experiences. We share ideas, our time, our love, and our trust.

I'm always moved by the biblical references to Abraham and Isaac walking together. God commanded Abraham to offer his son Isaac to him, and the Bible states that they embarked on a journey to Mount Moriah. Imagine the trepidation and uncertainty of the mission. What did God really want? How could God be asking Abraham to make such an ultimate sacrifice? The Bible states twice, "They walked together." One of the great Jewish commentators, Rashi, explains that they first walked together in body. They walked side by side but not with a united understanding of the mission ahead. When Isaac asked where the sacrificial ram was and Abraham responded, "God will show us," they again walked together with mutual understanding and trust. I can only imagine that no words were shared and the walk was in silence—but surely never forgotten.

Think about the walks you've taken in your life. Were they taken when holding your parents' or loved one's hand? Walking in the woods, in the snow or rain, somehow these moments stir joy in our souls. Thinking back on my life, I'll never forget the game I played with my youngest sister, Chanie, when we walked back from synagogue together on Saturdays. She would hold my hand and then I'd let go, run ahead, and she would chase me down. It was the only way I could get her to move faster.

I think of seizing the glory of a sparkling day and joining my children for a walk along the river in the Mianus River Gorge Preserve. Inevitably, I find that on these walks, we open up to each other, listen more acutely, and deepen our friendship and love.

Tool Box

❶ **Make it a habit to walk often with someone you love.**

❷ **In an interview with Alan Kalter,** the announcer of the *Late Show with David Letterman*, he shared with me the lasting memory of "walking to synagogue hand in hand with my papa, my father's father. I only did it a couple of times and I was probably five years old, six years old. I used to spend a week each summer with the two of them, my grandmother and grandfather, my grandma and papa. I continued to do that after my grandfather died when I was twelve." Take your child or grandchild on a walk to a place you love!

❸ **Try the "I'll never forget" exercise.** Write the words "I'll never forget" on the top of a page in your journal (or on a piece of paper) and think about the moments in your life that you'll never forget. Why do these thoughts emerge? How can you reverse engineer your life to live them now with someone you love?

A Timeless Touch and Memory of the Senses

It happened in the middle of the night in Jerusalem. I experienced a sensory flashback. As I stayed awake to care for my father in the hospital after his heart surgery, he asked me to rub his body down with cool water and a cloth. His blood temperature had dropped and he needed some relief. As my hand touched his cool skin, my mind flooded with memories of him holding me as a child in the deep water of a pool. I remembered so vividly my arms wrapped around his neck as he waded with me into the water.

As my father cared for me as a young boy, the touch reinforced for me my obligation as his child to care for him. One touch, impressed into the recesses of my soul, was awakened forty years later in life. What touch will you never forget? I remember the touch of my mother's hand for the very last time as she squeezed it in the hospital, letting me know she was aware of my presence, and the comfort of holding my wife Diane's hand for the first time.

The countless hugs of my parents, and mine to my children, convey a love, strength, and belief that always stay with me. As we reverse engineer our lives, think about the power of a touch to endure, to create a memory, and, most important, to enrich a relationship.

Tool Box

❶ **Hug your child, hug a friend.** Author and motivational speaker Leo Buscaglia says, "Too often we underestimate the power of a touch, a smile, a kind word, a listening ear, an honest compliment, or the smallest act of caring, all of which have the potential to turn a life around."

❷ **The poet John Keats wrote, "Touch has a memory."**
Reflect on the memory of a touch or holding hands.
When and who will you never forget? Why? How can you
re-create that feeling for another?

❸ **The scent of a soul:** The soul never forgets a smell.
Smell etches memories into our long-term memory bank
more than any of the other senses. The mystical roots of the
phenomenon stem from the beginning of time when God
breathed the breath of life into humanity. Until this day,
when I smell freshly baked bread or matzah ball soup, it
stirs within me warm memories of home and hearth. What
comfort foods do you serve to others? What family recipes
reflect your home and traditions? Make a homemade recipe.

Life moves at breakneck speed. We all wonder where the time
goes. No matter how much money we possess, we can't stop time.
We age. Yet every one of us possesses the capacity to bend the curve
and slow down time. It all depends on how we harness each moment
and our heightened awareness of the passage of time. Leonardo da
Vinci encapsulates this idea in his words: "In rivers, the water that you
touch is the last of what has passed and the first of that which comes;
so with present time." The principle of creating memories reflects the
gift of life. In every hour and in every day, through our love, generosity, time, and humanity, we can enrich our relationships and forge
an eternal legacy that is priceless. Review this chapter once a month.
Begin the practice of creating memories today. You'll bridge Heaven
and Earth, and ensure your legacy now and forever!

Celebrity Stirrings

We're human, which means we're mortal. Ultimately, the true testament to our eternity emerges from our impact on children, the future generation. In interviewing celebrities, I was moved by the spirit of Mayim Bialik (known to many from her title role in the television series *Blossom*), an American actress currently starring in *The Big Bang Theory* and nominated four times for the Primetime Emmy Award for outstanding supporting actress in a comedy series. Her life was shaped deeply by the memories of her parents, and she in turn strives to create such positive, life-affirming memories with her children. She understands the privilege and responsibility of being a parent and a role model:

I try to make every day an opportunity for us to see our children doing exceptional things. Having a feeling of satisfaction and purpose is not far away; it's in our hands. Of course, I want to do fun things with my kids, but I want them to remember what it feels like to help someone. My father was a drama teacher for most of my life, and he would go into special education classrooms and ask if any students wanted to be in the mainstream drama class. I remember when I was eight or nine crying with such joy to see deaf children signing to children who could hear.

To me that's what I try and do. I try to make every single day an opportunity for my children to do exceptional things. Whether it's picking up trash or giving money to someone who is hungry and begging for money on the side of the road, it's giving all those opportunities to show that the feeling of satisfaction and the feeling of purpose is not far. It's literally in their hands, right? I try and make sure, of course, that we do fun things with our kids. We actually just took a first real vacation with them. We went to Mexico for four days and we stopped by a pool. They may remember that, but I want them to remember feelings. I want them to remember what it feels like to help someone. I want them to remember when I hold them late at night and I put them to bed.

❧

*"Memories are the key not to the past
but to the future."*

—Corrie Ten Boom

CHAPTER 6

Principle No. 5:
Find Faith

I remember the moment as if it was yesterday. More than twenty-five years ago, sitting in DeKalb General Hospital in Atlanta next to my mother as she lay in a coma, I sensed this would be my last time in her physical presence. For the first twenty years of my life, she taught me, cared for me, loved me, and motivated me. I couldn't believe the reality we all faced. I felt the touch of her hand and offered her a kiss on the forehead. I looked at her, once so full of life and now barely holding on. I remember feeling such sadness and despair.

How could this have happened? How would we survive as a family? All I felt was the world caving in and a darkness enveloping me. I began to cry from the depths of my heart. The January day was cloudy and cold, as if the world mourned with me. I struggled to find an anchor, some ray of hope, some way to be able to move forward. My universe was turned upside down. My mother had died, and although I was surrounded by family and friends, I felt all alone.

In retrospect, I understand now that those days were a crucible of my faith. As a young boy, I believed in a higher power but was never before challenged to muster such strength. To this day, I remember making a choice: I could either believe my mother's untimely death was an accident and reject God or I could choose, in humility, to accept a higher plan and harness all of my inner strength, the resources of my faith, to carry my mother with me in soul and spirit and grow from this dark time in my life. I chose life and renewed my faith.

As a rabbi, husband, father, teacher, and friend, I realize that every day I'm faced with a choice to sit in the darkness or light a fire. We all are. But we all choose between despair and hope, regret or resolve, stagnation or growth.

Just as God proclaimed "Let there be light" in the midst of chaos and darkness at the beginning of time, we must confront moments of personal chaos, darkness, and spiritual stagnation and choose to instill our lives with clarity and light. We're tasked with the mission to find faith and see the light, and to pass the light to others.

This chapter offers you the fuel to fortify your faith on the journey of reverse engineering your life. You're reading this book because you truly desire a life of greater meaning and impact. We all do. We all possess dreams and aspirations.

However, before I talk about those moments when we seem to stagnate and lose the passion and sight for our aspirations, I want to dive deep into some of the truly existential questions we all might face at one time in our lives. For me, the days in the midst of grief in the wake of my mother's untimely death were my crucible of faith. All of us experience times in life when we feel as though we're walking in the valley of the shadow of death. We cry and wonder why the world seems to be falling apart in front of our eyes. Why did someone die? Why do we suffer? Why was the answer to our prayers a resounding "No!"?

I don't have the answers to those questions. No one does. As a rabbi, I'm confronted by the question of why bad things happen to good people all too often. Much has been written about the question of theodicy, the defense of God's omnipotence and goodness in the face of evil, but that's not our topic here. However, I'd be remiss if I didn't share one perspective from the Bible.

King David in Psalm 8 cries out to God, "My God, my God, why have you abandoned me?" He feels bereft of his faith and the Almighty's presence. Yet, in reality, the verse expresses another idea. The Hebrew word "Lamah" suggests David isn't wondering "why" but "what." He's not questioning the unknowable but yearning to discover some meaning and purpose amid his suffering. We'll rarely understand why a tragedy happens in our life, but we're called upon to somehow move forward and grow, to discover light in the midst of our personal darkness.

One of the foremost thinkers in this area was Viktor Frankl, an Austrian neurologist and psychiatrist, as well as a Holocaust survivor. Frankl was the founder of logotherapy and the author of *Man's Search for Meaning*. Some of his quotes serve as touchstones for confronting the most challenging moments in our lives. I share them with you for reflection. How may his words enable you to rise in times of despair?

"When we are no longer able to change a situation, we are challenged to change ourselves."

*"Everything can be taken from a man but one thing:
the last of the human freedoms—to choose
one's attitude in any given set of circumstances,
to choose one's own way."*

*"Life is never made unbearable by circumstances,
but only by lack of meaning and purpose."*

*"Our greatest freedom is the freedom
to choose our attitude."*

I began this chapter from the depths of my soul. With my mother's death, I experienced a spiritual earthquake and shuddered inside. Over the years, I have grown. There is still a hole in me and our family, but I've learned to transform the hole into a reservoir of never-ending strength and motivation.

When I reflect on the years since that day in Atlanta, I realize how grateful I am for staying true to the urgency of life, which I experienced in the immediate aftermath of my mother's untimely death. How do we harness the moments we all experience when we are awakened to the significance of each day and the purpose of life? *The principle of finding faith offers a path to transforming our heightened consciousness in a moment of crisis to a sustainable awareness of the opportunities and blessings of every day.*

Think back for a moment in your life when you were embarking on a new venture, starting a new school, making a move to a new home, or celebrating a milestone in your life. We look forward to the fresh opportunities for growth and success. We're excited for the future! Yet almost without exception, we fail to realize all of our hopes and dreams. Our challenges may be our own self-doubts, a crisis of faith, or a tragedy, or maybe they emerge from the inevitable bumps along the road. At those times, we lose sight of our initial plan. We wonder where the time went and how we were diverted from our inner compass and its guiding light. The bounce in our step is gone and we're dispirited.

It's no secret that millions of people encounter such a phenomenon every New Year. We develop resolutions for the next year and within a week or two revert to old habits. We lack the stick-to-itiveness to stay focused on our goals and become dispirited when we face a roadblock. We lack the passion to daily rise above the day-to-day monotony of our lives and stay committed to taking the steps that will help us achieve our goals.

Most of us get stuck after the first sign of resistance or failure. We may miss a day of fulfilling our new resolutions, which morphs into a week, and then we act in a way that doesn't represent our ideal selves. We lose confidence in our ability to bounce back and move forward. We get stuck in a rut.

Here's the secret to success: *Be prepared for the obstacles; they're part of life's journey.*

The Ethics of the Fathers teaches that it's not up to us to finish the task but we can't desist from starting. We don't control the world, although sometimes we think we can plan the future. We can try our best, as we should, but the more we can learn about harnessing the obstacles and turning them into opportunities, the better. The more we prepare for the circuitous path of life, and the more we learn how to find joy in the routine, the more we'll stay true to our deepest values and goals.

In essence, the aim of this entire book is to give you the clarity and passion to stay true to your life mission. Imagine if you could live every day awakened to your higher purpose and with a renewed energy for harnessing each day to its fullest. This is the ultimate goal, and I know you have it in you to live life on a higher plane.

How do we find this strength and courage? How do we develop a positive attitude? How do we sustain the momentum of reverse engineering our lives? The answer is in the principle of finding faith.

One of my favorite stories is about a group father/son camping trip. As the group hiked through the middle of the woods, they encountered a large boulder blocking the path. The fathers challenged their sons to use their resources to lift the heavy stone. One by one, each child struggled to lift the rock, but to no avail. Yet the fathers urged them on by saying, "You have to use all of your resources." Finally, when the sons were on the verge of despair, the fathers enlightened them that using all of their resources meant asking one another for help. In short order, the boys together lifted the boulder from the path. It was a life lesson never to be forgotten.

Are you harnessing all of your resources? The more you do, the more successful you'll be on your journey. You'll inevitably stumble, but you'll transcend the challenges ahead. The sources of our faith may be in a higher power, within ourselves, or in friends or a spouse who believes in us more than we believe in ourselves. We all need cheerleaders in life. Who are yours?

The goal of the principle of finding faith is to give you fuel for your journey. Imagine you are traveling in a car through a long stretch of road without a gas station. What do you do? Knowing that you won't be able to find gas along the way, you prepare for the long haul and fill up your car before embarking on the journey. Only then will you be able to reach your destination.

Thank God, we experience peak moments when our cups of blessing are full and life seems so right. However, we'll also experience challenges and letdowns, disappointments, conflict, and failures, which is the nature of life and the essence of humanity. Who among those reading this book has never experienced a roadblock or a cold reality? The mark of success is not perfection but our response to failure.

When I think about the challenges we inevitably face in life, I reflect on the words I often share with a young couple as they stand beneath the marital canopy, excited to embark on a new stage in life. Of course, on such an occasion, toasts are made celebrating the joy and love. We all hope and pray that the euphoria they feel at this moment continues to deepen and grow. But I always remind them that life will inevitably confront them with the slings and arrows of outrageous fortune. However, how we manage and transcend these challenges will determine the longevity, strength, and depth of the relationship.

I remind them of the eagle as a metaphor for life. How does an eagle meet the challenge of turbulent winds? Head-on. Eagles love the storm. When clouds gather, the eagle gets excited and uses the storm's winds to lift it higher. The winds create lifting power in the thermal updrafts. The eagle reaches greater heights when he soars with them. In life, when we face our challenges and grow through them, we become even stronger and even learn to relish them.

The obstacles we face are actually opportunities for growth. American author and pastor John Maxwell characterizes this strategy as "failing forward." Thousands of years before him, King Solomon, the wisest of all men, reflected in Proverbs, "A righteous man falls seven times and gets up." In this chapter, you'll learn how to:

1. Renew faith in yourself by recognizing your potential.
2. Develop faith in the future and live life with optimism.
3. Find faith in a higher power and transform obstacles into opportunities.
4. Draw strength and courage from friends and share your dreams.

I have no doubt that you're reading this book with the best of intentions. You want spiritual greatness. You want to share your light. You want to deepen relationships, be your very best, and make a difference in the world every day. Join me as we explore the principle of finding faith. It's the secret to truly making your deepest aspirations come true.

Foundations

Believing in Yourself: Your Infinite Value

You can change. Every day is a new opportunity for growth. This may seem obvious, but Rabbi Yisrael Salanter once shared that it is easier to study the entire corpus of the Talmud than it is to change one character trait. The first day of a new program for spiritual growth is relatively easy, but as the routine sets in, we often lose our enthusiasm and revert to old habits. Without intent and thought, we automatically operate within our comfort zone. We don't push beyond our boundaries and, in short order, we relegate ourselves to the path of least spiritual resistance. Over the course of our lives, we never fully realize our potential.

Think about it this way. We all recognize the importance of physical exercise for developing our health and strengthening our bodies.

When we get on the treadmill, we start at a low resistance until we build our bodies up to be able to run faster. If we stayed at a pace of twelve-minute miles and never ran farther or faster, we wouldn't improve, and, in fact, our muscles would atrophy. Our character works the same way. We each possess a soul, a spark of the divine, an inner voice motivating us to make good choices and live out our deepest dreams and aspirations. It's a "soul muscle." Like the body, it must be challenged to grow stronger. When we stumble and perhaps don't achieve our goals on the first try, it's not time to give up but to grow up. It's not productive to look back and lament our failings but to push forward and start anew.

Every morning, God renews his faith in us. He breathes into us a new spirit. One of my favorite songs from my youth draws from the words of King David in Psalm 51. He acknowledges that God implanted a pure heart within each of us and prays that God renews his spirit within us every day. Whether you believe in God, you'll likely agree that the very act of arising in the morning reflects a state of new consciousness. You're alive today for a purpose. Don't lament days lost but seize the moment now to make the best of today.

It's no wonder that Moses in his final address to the Jewish people at the very end of his life consistently invoked the word "today" and "life." He said, "Today, I place before you the choice between life and death and good and evil. Choose life so you and your children will live."

Listen for a moment. What is Moses telling us? If we had a choice between life and death, wouldn't we choose life? Yet he challenges us to choose life. I think herein lies the essence of leading the type of life now for how you want to be remembered, and one of eternal significance. Choose life.

> *"Write it on your heart that every day*
> *is the best day in the year."*
>
> —Ralph Waldo Emerson

This choice is one we're called upon to make every day. For any of us to say, "This is who I am and this is who I will be" is an abdication of choosing life. No matter what age, when we grow, we live, and when we stagnate, we die. One of my mentors, Rabbi Aharon Lichtenstein, reflected, "The significance of having aspirations and dreams is critical. We should not subscribe to the conception that it is better to have minimal aspirations so as to have maximal contentment. The moral life, the spiritual life, the religious life, is one of yearning and aspiration."

One night on a television program, Rocky Marciano, the former heavyweight champion from 1952–56, who was undefeated in his career, was asked about the secret of his success. He replied, "I was hungry. I was always hungry." When Albert Einstein was asked about his goal in formulating the theory of relativity, he responded, "I challenged the axioms. To make a goal of comfort and happiness has never appealed to me." Our highest goals shouldn't be luxury or ease but accomplishment and becoming our best. If we don't move forward, we move backward. If we rest, we rust.

One of the most important steps on your journey is truly mobilizing the present moment to unleash your divine light. If you're reading this book, it's proof that God believes in you. He gave you health today and the gift of life for a higher purpose. Jewish mysticism teaches that all of our souls are endowed with a spark of the divine corresponding to each day of our lives. Each spark possesses potential that can only be harnessed on that day and no other. Once the day is gone, we've lost the opportunity to redeem the spark. What you do today couldn't have been achieved yesterday nor will you be able to do what you can do today tomorrow. As the great mystic the Baal Shem Tov wrote, "The ideal of man is to be a revelation himself, clearly to recognize himself as a manifestation of God." Your potential is infinite. Never give up on yourself. God won't, and neither should you.

One of the most moving stories reflecting the importance of forgiving ourselves and believing in our future is from a little book entitled *The Language of Faith* by Robert Dewey. A man and a boy, in a lonely vigil, share a seat on a train ride to a small town called Smithville.

The man first notices the boy when he is coming down the aisle and, when the train gives a great lurch, he finds himself flung into an unoccupied aisle seat next to the boy. Surprise cannot hide the anxiety on the boy's face.

"How old is the boy?" the man asks himself. "Is he seventeen or eighteen? What could worry someone so young?"

The man is thinking, "The look on the boy's face is not easy to explain. Is it shame or guilt? Whatever it is, the boy's tension is obvious. He pays no attention to any passerby."

The man wonders if the boy is looking outside but he peers out the window and sees nothing. The man tries to forget the boy by opening up a magazine, but looks up to see the boy's head drop dejectedly against the window. He notices that the hand against the window is clenched into a fist. The man feels sure the boy is fighting from crying.

The man begins to read and the boy sits quietly. Every now and then the boy steals a look at the man instead of peering out the window. Finally, the boy asks the man if he knows what time it is and when the train will get to Smithville. The man gives him the time, but he does not know the arrival time in Smithville. "That's where you're headed?" he asks the boy. "Yes," the boy replies.

"It's a very small town, isn't it?" replies the man. "I didn't realize the train stopped there."

"It doesn't usually, but they said they would stop for me," says the boy. "You live there do you?" said the man. "Yes, that is, I used to." "Going back then?" "Yes, that is, I think so . . . maybe?" The questions turn the boy back to the window. It is quite a while before he speaks again. When he does, it is to tell the story of his life.

Four years ago, he had done something so wrong that he ran away from home. He couldn't face his father, and he had left without telling anyone. Since then, he had worked here and there, but never for long in one place. He had learned about the pain in life and he had often been without money. Sometimes he was very sick, usually very lonely, and once in a while very close to real trouble.

Finally, he had decided to go home to his father's house. For a while that is all the boy says. The man doesn't press him with questions, but finally he asked just one. "Does your father know you're coming?" "Yes!" replies the boy. "Then he will be there to meet you, I imagine."

"Maybe, I don't know." Silence again . . . and a long look out the window . . . then the rest of the story. "I don't know if he wants me back after what I did. I'm not sure he can ever forgive me. He has never known where I was all this time, and I've never written to him, except for a letter I wrote three days ago in which I said I would be coming home. I know how much I hurt him . . . he must have been very hurt.

"In the letter I said I would be coming home if he wanted me to. There's a tree a few hundred feet beside the little station in Smithville. We used to climb it all of the time . . . my older brother and me. In the letter, I told my dad to put a sign on the tree if he wanted me to get off the train and come home. I told him I'd look for a white ribbon on one of the branches that hangs over the fence where the train passes. So, if there's a ribbon on the tree, I'll get off. If there isn't, I'll ride to somewhere else. I don't know where."

The train rushes on through the night and once again the conversation wanes. A kind of silent companionship has developed between the man and boy; both are now waiting for Smithville. Suddenly, the boy turns from the window and speaks with such intensity that it takes the man by surprise. "Will you look for me? I'm sort of scared! All of a sudden I don't know what to expect." "Sure. I'll be glad to," the man replies.

They change seats. Shortly after the man had begun to peer into the darkness, the conductor comes through announcing, "Smithville! Next stop!" The boy makes no move. He says nothing. He merely drops his head into his hands waiting. The man peers into the darkness. Then he sees it. He shouts so loudly that everyone in the car can hear him. "Son! The tree is covered with white ribbons!"[10]

Never give up. Rise above your seeming limitations and recognize your unbounded personal potential. God loves you.

I'm moved by the inspiring story of Dr. Rahamim Melamed-Cohen, who has a PhD in special education, held a leading position in Israel's Ministry of Education, served as head of the Education Department in a Jerusalem college, and pioneered special education programs throughout Israel. At fifty-seven, a husband, father of six children, and grandfather to many grandchildren, he was diagnosed with Lou Gehrig's disease.

The doctor told him, "You have three to five years to live." That was fourteen years ago. Three of the doctors who attended him have since died, but Melamed-Cohen, while completely paralyzed, is still going strong. Since the onset of his illness, he has written seven books, the latest by means of a computer that types by his eye movements.

He didn't get to his present state of serene acceptance immediately. A religious man, when he first heard the diagnosis, he had many questions for God: "Why did this happen to me? What did I do wrong?" As his physical condition has deteriorated, his faith has grown stronger. He notices in himself the spiritual growth spawned by his illness: "I think I understand better than most people how to appreciate the important things in life, and to ignore those things that aren't important."

Yet, with all his preparations, he didn't prepare for the inevitable moment that strikes all ALS sufferers: the final moment when the paralysis creeps into the lungs. One day, eight years ago, his wife, Elisheva, heard her husband straining to breathe. She called an ambulance. The medics arrived at the same moment that his breathing stopped. They resuscitated him and rushed him to the hospital. There Elisheva made the decision to hook her husband up to a respirator rather than let him die.

"Everything would have been different in one minute," Elisheva recalls, "if I hadn't called the ambulance. And there was a doctor in the emergency room who said to me, 'Why did you resuscitate him?' This was very terrible to hear."

When he regained consciousness, Melamed-Cohen himself was not sure that being kept alive by a respirator was the best decision. Now, however, he asserts, "If they had let me die, I would have missed the best and most important years of my life."

His daily struggle with survival has taught him a vital lesson about the vast, untapped potential inherent in every person. "Before, I didn't believe that I have such inner strength. I learned that every human being has sparks that he can transform into a burning flame."

He runs a small school founded by his late father. This entails determining the curriculum, examining the applicants, paying the staff, and keeping daily track of the attendance and progress of each student. He also reads books and newspapers. Twice a week he has physiotherapy. At 4:00 p.m., visitors start arriving—his four siblings, six children, twenty-six grandchildren, friends, or former colleagues.

Melamed-Cohen is an example for all people who feel that they can't get on with their lives because of something they're lacking: a spouse, children, money, a fulfilling job, health, and so on. Although lacking many rudimentary functions, he advises, "Don't despair. Be optimistic and work on joy in your heart. No matter what you are lacking, think of what is possible to do in your present situation."

Melamed-Cohen's life is animated by his desire to disseminate this message to the world. When asked what his plans for the future are, he responded, "I want to stay alive for many more years and not miss out on even one moment of my life. I want the opportunity to actualize the true me, to enjoy others and to be enjoyed by others, and to convey the message of optimism and that life is holy."

A searing segment of the film *Heroes Against Their Will* shows Melamed-Cohen debating with Dr. Noam Reches, the chairman of the Israel Medical Ethics Committee and a leading proponent of euthanasia, who himself has "pulled the plug" on request. Dr. Reches looks at the wheelchair-bound Melamed-Cohen, with the respirator tube connected to the tracheotomy in his neck, and says, "You can't feed yourself. You can't hug the people you love. If I were in your position, I'd want out." Melamed-Cohen responds, "These are the most beautiful and happiest years of my life."

Read the words of Helen Keller and allow her and Melamed-Cohen's spirit to penetrate your heart: "I have for many years endeavored to make this vital truth clear; and still people marvel when I tell them that I am happy. They imagine that my limitations weigh heavily upon my spirit, and chain me to the rock of despair. Yet, it seems to me, happiness has very little to do with the senses. If we make up our minds that this is a drab and purposeless universe, it will be that, and nothing else. On the other hand, if we believe that the earth is ours, and that the sun and moon hang in the sky for our delight, there will be joy upon the hills and gladness in the fields because the Artist in our souls glorifies creation. Surely, it gives dignity to life to believe that we are born into this world for noble ends, and that we have a higher destiny than can be accomplished within the narrow limits of this physical life."

Thoughts and Actions Affect Emotions: Living Life with Optimism

Finding faith is also about cultivating an optimistic spirit. How do we stay positive? How do we cultivate hope? The road to your heart is through your head and your hands. What we think and say affects our emotional state, and so does what we do.

I'm a firm believer that what goes into your head will affect your heart. It's true, as author and motivational speaker Zig Ziglar declared, that your attitude will determine your altitude. William James, the noted American philosopher and psychologist, developed an idea in his book *The Will to Believe*. He wrote, "The greatest discovery of my generation is that a human being can alter his life by altering his attitudes."

I credit my mother and father with instilling within me a can-do approach to life and the value of positive thinking. I learned not only from their words but their deeds as well. As parents, our children learn from how we respond to setbacks. Do we blame others for our disappointments, or as my father always says, "When one door closes, another door opens." My mother's motto, when asked how she was doing no matter the chaos in the house—"Thank God, I am fantastic!"—lifted my spirits and buoys me to this day.

When asking my father about the roots of his positive spirit, he shared that much of it was shaped by his teachers at Yeshiva University. The stories in the Bible, as explored by his mentors, served as touchstones of faith. It reminded me of the most moving stories of living with optimism. Jacob, fearing for his life, as Esau threatened to murder him, fled from home. He was weak in spirit and filled with anxiety. While asleep on the road, he dreamed of angels ascending and descending a ladder and God appeared to him and promised that he would not abandon him. Upon hearing the promise of protection, the Bible states enigmatically that Jacob's heart lifted his feet rather than stating that Jacob walked away. The medieval commentator Rashi said that the odd formulation reflects a change in Jacob's mental state and psychology. Before the promise, he was fearful and scared, and now God's words to him literally filled his heart, captured his spirit, lifted his feet, and gave him a spring in his step.

On your road to leading a life of impact, you'll also be dissuaded. You'll likely get down and feel lethargy in your step. What gives you your sense of optimism and positive outlook on life? These sources of inspiration will be invaluable to you.

I've discovered that when you offer positive words to someone else, when you give someone a needed emotional boost, you yourself are uplifted. People will often ask me how I'm able, as a rabbi, to give people comfort in times of grief and tragedy. They ask, "Isn't it emotionally draining? What do you say when you walk into a house of sorrow? How do you comfort the bereaved?" I know that I can't provide answers to why something has happened, but I can provide strength and hope. From my heart, I share that God will give them strength and that I and others are there for them. Just being present, sharing a kind word, and praying with them in turn renews my strength. As Saint Francis of Assisi wrote, "For it is in giving that we receive."

It's not only our words but our actions that affect our emotions. Just when you feel you can't go on, you don't have it in you, push forward. In the words of William James, "Act as if what you do makes a difference. It does."

The amazing story of Charles Blondin, a famous French tightrope walker, illustrates the true nature of faith. Blondin's greatest fame came on September 14, 1860, when he became the first person to cross a tightrope stretched 11,000 feet (more than a quarter of a mile) across the mighty Niagara Falls. People from Canada and America came from miles away to see this great feat.

He walked across, 160 feet above the falls, several times, each time with a different, daring feat: once in a sack, on stilts, on a bicycle, in the dark, and blindfolded. One time he even carried a stove and cooked an omelet in the middle of the rope! A large crowd gathered and the buzz of excitement ran along both sides of the riverbank. The crowd oohed and aahed as Blondin carefully walked across—one dangerous step after another—pushing a wheelbarrow holding a sack of potatoes.

Then at one point, he asked for the participation of a volunteer. Upon reaching the other side, the crowd's applause was louder than the roar of the falls! Blondin suddenly stopped and addressed his audience: "Do you believe I can carry a person across in this wheelbarrow?" The crowd enthusiastically yelled, "Yes! You are the greatest tightrope walker in the world. We believe!"

"Okay," said Blondin, "who wants to get into the wheelbarrow?"

Do you believe in thought or also in deed? Henry Ford said, "You can't build a reputation on what you are going to do." We can say all we want—that we want to become better people, that we want to spend more time with family, put first things first in our lives, and not wait for a moment of awakening—but until we act, our thoughts and words are merely lip service. We aren't judged by what we say but what we do and how we lead our lives. Do good and you'll be good and feel good. Even if you don't feel like doing a kind deed, even if you're dissuaded, put one foot in front of the next and move forward.

I call this dimension of faith "walking in the water." The timeless biblical story of the Exodus from Egypt provides the basis for this idea. When the Jewish people were standing at the Sea of Reeds, with the Egyptians behind them and the deep waters in front of them, they cried out to God for help. "Save us," they pleaded. God informed Moses that now was not the time to pray but the time to act. He told him to walk into the water and take the first step. One man, Nachshon, the leader of Judah, walked in until the water reached his neck. He didn't know if he would survive. At the last moment, God split the water. God was waiting for him to act courageously, for mankind to take the first steps, and the Almighty revealed the dry land.

Your path to reverse engineering your life will sometimes necessitate walking in the water. You won't know the fruits of your labors or be inspired to forge ahead until you actually step out in faith. Remember the wisdom of the Ethics of the Fathers: "It is not up you to finish the task but you are not free therefore from trying."

> *"Jump, and you will find out how to*
> *unfold your wings as you fall."*
>
> —Ray Bradbury

Many years ago, my youngest sister Chanie was diagnosed with multiple sclerosis. She was newly married, but she found the strength and spirit to forge head and find faith within. She recently wrote this article on the website *Mother Nature Network*, which exemplifies finding faith.

The date was February 14, 2007—Valentine's Day. It started off like any other morning. I had been seeing my doctor for about a month for a strange weak feeling in my leg. First, he suggested a nerve test to make sure I was feeling everything properly. Then he did some blood work. Next, he did an MRI. I don't know why none of this stuff fazed me, but it didn't. I was wholly unprepared for what was to come next.

It had started to snow—a light snowfall—at my home in Elizabeth, New Jersey. I had a doctor's appointment in Teaneck (about a half hour away) with a neurologist—I assumed just to discuss the next steps to figure out what was causing the rather mild weakness I was feeling. My husband was working from home that day, and I decided to drive myself to the doctor. Even though it was snowing, Teaneck was home to my favorite coffee shop. Maybe I would stop in for a coffee and a muffin on the way home, a little treat on a frigid morning. I was blissfully unaware of what today would bring.

I got to the doctor's office a little after 10:00 a.m. and flipped through magazines in the waiting room. When I was finally brought to the little room to wait for him, I started to get a bit nervous. Everyone around here was so serious.

The doctor walked in, after what felt like an eternity, with three binders and started going over treatment options. Treatment options.

My head started to spin. I stopped the doctor midsentence as he was explaining the side effects of a certain drug and asked him why he was showing me all this stuff. Did I miss something? "You have multiple sclerosis," he replied. "Nobody told you?"

I don't know how I made it through the rest of the appointment. Especially when the receptionist said on my way out, "Glad you could make it. I'm sorry it's MS," as if she had just told me she didn't have change for a twenty.

All I remember was stumbling outside, into the freezing temperatures, and trying to clear off my snow-covered car through stinging, hot tears. I breathlessly jammed my husband's number into my cell phone and told him I had multiple sclerosis. He was so confused.

Driving home was a blur. The roads were icy. My eyes were hot with tears. I was sobbing. I almost spun out a few times and thought about what would happen if I died right then and there. When I arrived home, I collapsed into my husband's arms, convulsing in tears. How could this be happening to me? I felt like I was suffocating. I was only twenty-six. My life was perfect. What happened?

Ever since my mom died suddenly when I was eight years old, I had always thought I had been given a free pass to a great life. I mean, what else could go wrong? That was pretty bad, right? And then this happened. I honestly don't remember much of the rest of the day, but I know I spent most of it in tears, feeling sorry for myself.

Over the next few months, with the help of excellent neurologists (not including the one I saw above), I learned about my disease. I learned that it wasn't a death sentence. I learned how to advocate for myself medically, since no one else would. I learned that getting a second opinion, and even a third, is more than okay when it comes to your health. And I also learned that the ones who really care stick by you.

I consider myself blessed. Blessed because my multiple sclerosis isn't so bad. I can walk, I can run, I can dance. And I do. I am also blessed because I live with the sense of urgency that most people live with only after something terrible happens. You know that feeling you get when you hear about a young child dying tragically? The one that makes you want to hug your children or call your spouse and tell them you love them? I live with that feeling every day. Sure, it comes with its setbacks. I am that mom who constantly thinks something terrible is about to happen. I see a mild rash on my daughter and my mind immediately jumps to cancer. I hear my son cough in his sleep and I think he must be choking. Sure, I'm a bit of an alarmist. But that's what comes with having a disease that could literally leave me helpless at any moment. I am blessed. No matter what may happen tomorrow, I am blessed right now. Sometimes (more often than I'd like) I have to tell myself that. But in the moments that I just remember it, I am truly happy.

I used to have a saying on my fridge from an evangelical pastor named Charles Swindoll. The quote is a general one about having a positive attitude in life, but one line has always resonated with me. It reads, "Life is 10 percent what happens to you and 90 percent how you react to it." We all have struggles. I know I do. But life is all about having a positive attitude and living each day to its fullest, so that when it is our last, we can look back with no regrets.

Faith in a Higher Power: Diversions or Destiny

The most essential ingredient for spiritual success and leading a life of eternal impact is how you view and navigate the detours and disappointments in your journey. I can guarantee you that all of your plans will not come to fruition. You need to set goals and do your best to stay focused on achieving them, but life is not fully in your control. None of us can anticipate the end results of all of our efforts. Having faith means starting a task even though you may not get to finish it. It means celebrating and harnessing the sparks in every day.

All too often, we lament the fact that we can't achieve our goals because of an external circumstance: this person didn't return my call; if only I was in a better business; if I lived someplace else, my life would be easy; when I get this promotion, then I'll have time for the important values in my life; when I reach this milestone, then I'll be in a position to devote more time to my family. Yet when we only see life's problems, we never realize the infinite possibilities latent in each day and hour.

The Ethics of the Fathers teaches that there is no human being who doesn't have his hour and place. It's possible for a person to have lived more than seventy years and not yet fulfilled their mission. The obstacles we encounter are designed for growth. To realize your hopes, find ways to accept the reality you face and garner the courage to make the moment great and memorable every day. Your life will be transformed with this attitude.

This philosophy of life is inspired by the belief that there is a divine design to every second of the day. There is a higher power. No diversion is without merit and meaning. Find your destiny and transform the obstacles into an opportunity. If you meet someone, there is a holy purpose in the encounter. If you experience a closed door and a lost opportunity, know that you're being pushed to find another opening in your life that you never thought possible.

The concept is radical but it will change your life forever. No moment is for naught; no encounter is random. You find faith when you realize that within each moment is infinite potential for growth and change. *When you find yourself seemingly off your projected path, rather than mourn, find meaning.* When you can adapt in this way, you'll discover new joy in life and realize new horizons and holiness.

Who will join you on your journey? Everyone needs a cheerleader. We can all identify people in our lives who give us good advice or push us when we need it most. We all need partners, mentors, and friends. Who are yours? My brother Elie shared a story with me about an amazing run at the 1991 US Open by Jimmy Connors. At thirty-nine, everyone assumed he was over the hill, incapable of victory, yet he won a number of matches, much to everyone's surprise, and made it to the semifinals. When asked how he overcame the odds, he responded, "When you hear thirty thousand people cheering, 'Jimmy, Jimmy,' how can you not be lifted? How can you not respond?"

If thirty thousand screaming fans are enough to lift a thirty-nine-year-old tennis player, how much more can a cheer from God boost us to new heights?

In Psalm 27:10, King David said, "Even if my mother and father have abandoned me, God will gather me in," and the concluding lines of the psalm focus on asking God to renew his faith and strength.

When interviewing Ron Howard, he shared the importance of mentors in his life. An actor rarely transitions successfully to becoming a director. He told me, "I am deeply grateful to the people in my life who have listened to me and given me wisdom. I had a great history teacher, coaches, and people in entertainment who really tried to understand my questions and give me guidance. I know a handful of people who, without my knowing it, early in my career gave some character references for me. Kid actors don't generally have adult careers. People thought my idea to go into a sitcom was adorable.

I had people who had just the right things to say to me at the right time. Their wisdom was not easy to hear, but they definitely helped me at moments of crossroads in my personal and professional life."

Take people with you on your journey. Use all of your resources as you reverse engineer your life. Your biggest support may be a friend, a mentor, or a higher power—or all of them. Finding faith in yourself, in a higher power, and in your friends and family will fortify you for the journey to become your very best!

Strategies

Talk to Your Inner Child

One of my heroes is Elie Wiesel, a Romanian-born Jewish writer, professor, political activist, Holocaust survivor, and Nobel Laureate. In his acceptance speech in Oslo, December 10, 1986, he spoke of the roots of his lifelong passion for justice and the fight against evil in the world. In his words lay one of the most important strategies for keeping the faith and living life with purpose and responsibility. Out of the ashes of the Holocaust, he mustered the courage to find meaning and mission. He understood his responsibility to his inner child. He shared the following:

> It is with a profound sense of humility that I accept the honor you have chosen to bestow upon me. I know: your choice transcends me. . . . It pleases me because I may say that this honor belongs to all the survivors and their children, and through us, to the Jewish people with whose destiny I have always identified.
>
> I remember: it happened yesterday or eternities ago. A young Jewish boy discovered the kingdom of night. I remember his bewilderment, I

remember his anguish. It all happened so fast. The ghetto. The deportation. The sealed cattle car. The fiery altar upon which the history of our people and the future of mankind were meant to be sacrificed.

I remember: he asked his father: "Can this be true?" This is the twentieth century, not the Middle Ages. Who would allow such crimes to be committed? How could the world remain silent?

And now the boy is turning to me: "Tell me," he asks. "What have you done with my future? What have you done with your life?"

And I tell him that I have tried. That I have tried to keep memory alive, that I have tried to fight those who would forget. Because if we forget, we are guilty, we are accomplices. We must always take sides. Neutrality helps the oppressor, never the victim. Silence encourages the tormentor, never the tormented.[11]

The world is a better place because of Elie Wiesel's unyielding passion toward his past. He lived with a supreme sense of responsibility to the child of his youth. He found faith arising from the darkness of the Holocaust.

What would your future self say to you today? As children, we're all dreamers. We possess hopes for a brighter future. Have you let those childhood dreams die? We age and our bodies are different now than twenty, thirty, or forty years ago. Yet we must never abandon the promises of our youth. Our souls are timeless and eternal. Don't let the sometimes cold and harsh reality of life dampen your dreams. Push through the obstacles.

Remind yourself how in the heat, your first reaction may be to get out of it, but in the end, sometimes it's only in the crucible that we grow.

Tool Box

❶ **Write a letter to your future self:** Date it today and choose a date one, five, or ten years down the road. You may even choose to write a letter in monthly increments. When you open it in the future, allow the words to seep into your consciousness and awaken you to your inner hopes and dreams. Did you stay true to them? How can you get back on track?

❷ **Draw your dreams:** What would it look like if you were living your dreams? If you had a magic wand, what would you change about your life?

❸ **Daring to dream:** What would you do if you were not afraid? What would fearlessness look like?

Sharing Your Dreams

Life is not meant to be lived alone. Just as you want to make the most of every day and develop yourself and strengthen your relationships, others do too. I believe that we're all created with strengths and weaknesses so we can search out others with whom we can collaborate. Take people on the journey with you. About ten years ago, I learned the importance of sharing your dreams. I joined a leadership seminar entitled "From Good to Great," and at the end we crafted a wooden box and made physical reminders of our lessons learned. For me, I realized that in order to fulfill my mission in the world, I needed to share. What comes from the heart will go into someone else's heart. People sense authenticity. They in turn will reveal their

dreams and together you may discover a kindred spirit with whom
you can realize your dreams.

Tool Box

❶ **Identify one person who you trust and who truly desires to
see you fulfilled in life.** Share your plan to reverse engineer
your life.

❷ **Identify a mentor in your professional life.** Schedule an
initial meeting. Seek their guidance. Stay in touch on a
consistent basis.

❸ **How can your dream be a gift to yourself, your family,
or your community?** Share your ideas with a few people;
explore other dreams and hopes for your community and
family, and seek out ways to realize them.

Opening Your Eyes with Joy

How do we gain a perspective of joy and find faith in ourselves?
How do we stay motivated to believe that each day has an inherent
gift for growth? It starts with the moment you open your eyes. What
are the first words you say when you wake up in the morning? Zig
Ziglar once commented that every morning, we're faced with two
choices—to wake up to an alarm clock or an opportunity clock. Do
we press snooze or do we seize the day?

Every morning when I wake up, I offer the following prayer: "God,
the soul you instilled within me is pure. You created me and you
breathed into me the spirit of life. Great is your faith in me." The
way you begin your day frames your attitude toward what lies ahead.

Wow! I can talk, I can walk, and I can hear the sounds outside and smell the fresh air. If God infuses each of us with new life today, we in turn must relish the chance to make the day a masterpiece!

Tool Box

❶ Body scan: When you wake up, take four deep breaths. Close your eyes and place your attention on your toes; be present with how they feel. Then slowly move your awareness up from your feet to your legs, through your hips, torso, arms, chest, neck, and head, always staying present with the sensations in each part of your body. Once you reach your head, move your awareness back down your body, feeling each limb internally and imagining white light flowing through your body (for more ideas, see "5 Easy Rituals to Start Your Day with Energy & Joy," available at *http://www.mindbodygreen.com/0-16936/5-easy-rituals-to-start-your-day-with-energy-joy.html*).

❷ Thank you: When you open your eyes, express your gratitude for three gifts in your life.

❸ Mission possible: Each of us can accomplish something significant every day. What is your sacred mission today? How will you make the world better? Missions motivate!

Reframing

Turn your obstacles into opportunities. My father and mother always taught me that when one door closes another opens. God possesses a higher plan for us. In *The Power of Positive Thinking*, Norman

Vincent Peale shared a threefold prayer (which he had learned from a salesman) that encapsulates the spirit of reframing. The guy originally could never seem to hold a job for more than a year, and then he received the following prayer, which, when recited every day, changed his mental attitude and sowed success in his life: "I believe I am divinely guided. I believe I will always take the right turn in the road. I believe that God will always make a way when there is no way." Never accept defeat. With God everything is possible. The pushback you experience is your gateway to infinite possibilities. Remember the words of Isaiah 40:31: "They that wait upon the Lord shall renew their strength; they shall mount up with wings as eagles; they shall run, and not be weary; and they shall walk, and not faint."

Tool Box

❶ **Turn "I can't" into "I will":** Make a list of all the things you "can't" do. We all have hundreds. Evaluate them and distinguish between "I can't" and "I don't feel like it." Consider the list and commit to turning the "I can't" into "I will."

❷ **Remind yourself of open doors:** Identify personal examples of when a seeming obstacle or "closed door" revealed a new and exciting opportunity. Make it a weekly practice.

❸ **Develop happiness skills:** Try the one-hour blessing fest. Spend one hour writing everything for which you are grateful. The first twenty minutes is easy, but stay with the exercise for the entire time. It'll force you to look at your life as never before.

"Every wall is a door."

—Ralph Waldo Emerson

Daily Inspiration

The process of reverse engineering your life begins with the belief that you possess the capacity to change. It's rooted in the fundamental idea that every day we can choose our actions. We can learn from our mistakes, take responsibility for the past, and act differently. This might seem obvious, but in truth, subconsciously the forces of stagnation emerge. Just as we strive for a physical workout every day to keep our bodies in good health, we need to strive to strengthen our spirit every day. Here are a few ideas for spiritual rejuvenation.

Tool Box

❶ **Read a passage or chapter from the Psalms every day.**
I recently adopted this practice and it has changed my life. I feel refreshed every day with a renewed sense of purpose. I sense God at my side every day. Mariano Rivera, one of baseball's greatest pitchers, loves the book of Psalms. It reinforces his belief that God gave him certain talents to use. He shared, "Not to bring glory to Mariano Rivera but to the Lord."

❷ **Sign up online to daily doses of inspiration.**

❸ **Create daily reminder cards of character goals and read one when you awake in the morning.** (Examples: "Peace—Rise Above the Inconsequential" or "Kindness—Bring Light into a Corner of Darkness," or create your own.)

❹ **Surround yourself with positive influences** (Psalm 101:3:
"I will not set before my eyes anything that is worthless.
I hate the work of those who fall away; it shall not cling
to me"). Choose wisely the books you read, the music you
listen to, and the movies you watch. Spend time with
positive people.

Never lose hope. I truly believe that the best is yet to come in
your life. God renews creation every day and you're a part of that.
He believes in you and your capacity for greatness and leading a life
of eternal impact. Wherever you may be emotionally or spiritually,
today is a new day. Today, choose life.

Celebrity Stirrings

The world changed forever on 9/11. As in earlier generations
when no one could forget where they were when they heard of John
F. Kennedy's assassination, we all remember where we were when
the Twin Towers collapsed in the wake of terror attacks. It was a
dark time for our country and the world. Yet the country and its cit-
izens unified and found faith, friendship, and fortitude in the ensuing
weeks. One of the pivotal leaders during that time was Mayor Rudy
Giuliani. When interviewing him, he reflected on the role of Father
Mychal Judge in his life, the first person whom he learned died on
September 11. His reflection speaks of not only finding faith personally but the power we each possess to provide strength and renewed
faith to others.

Father Mychal was a Franciscan priest. He was the chaplain of the New York City Fire Department, and he died on September 11 at the site. For eight years he was with me at many, many, many of the Fire Department tragedies, and helped me through them. He also helped me through some of my personal issues in my life. He would offer advice. He would send me notes, telling me what a good person I was when I was being attacked in the press. He would leave me a note saying, "I know you're really upset about those articles in the paper today, but I remember you spent twelve hours at firefighter so-and-so's bedside with him, with me." He said, "Nobody else really knows that except you and me and God, and after all, the last one is the only important one."

On September 11, when I was notified that he was dead, and he was the first notification I got of a person who had died, there was a tremendous feeling of loss in the pit of my stomach. I was already thinking about the fact, because I had been told that maybe twelve thousand people were dead. I was thinking about who I was going to get to help me do this.

I was about to say to my fire commissioner, "Get me Father Judge," because I wanted him with me so I could start talking to him about what I was going to say, how I was going to say it, how I was going to treat these people. How much detail should I give them? How much detail should I spare them?

When I heard he was dead, I had the following feeling; it was almost like this, "You're on your own." "You've got to do it yourself." I thought, *Wow, I hope I can do this. I hope I can do this without him.* I was compassionate and said the right things at funerals and memorials; I probably went to a hundred all together. I learned most of that from him.

The most important wisdom he gave me was "Don't worry about what you say; just hug 'em. Sometimes we get too caught up with trying to find the right words to say." He said, "When somebody just lost their father and it's a ten-year-old boy, what are you going to say to them other than hugging them?" He said, "Once you hug them and you connect, you'll find the right words to say."

With firefighters' and police officers' families, it's always very helpful to focus on the aspect of courage and duty and choices, because in a way they chose this kind of life, and what heroes they are, and how we couldn't live without them. How our society would be so different. There are wonderful things you can say that sometimes don't connect immediately because the person is in such pain, but you know in most cases this is ultimately going to connect. You may say it today, and it may have meaning five days later.

I found the most difficult part of September 11 was talking to the families of what I would call the civilians. My administrative assistant brought us a coffee, and all of a sudden, we're all dead. Exactly why did we die? They weren't like Stephen Siller, the firefighter who ran from Brooklyn to New York and ran into the building and saved people. He made a choice to help people. He laid down his life to save others. These other people were just opening their computers. That was harder.

I truly believe the good will ultimately overcome evil. I think that even when I look at September 11, and I look at all the evil, terrible things. Then I look at how the city came together, the country came together, the tower's been rebuilt. Twice as many people live in lower Manhattan now than did before. I think good has won out over evil.

I think that the goals of the terrorists didn't prevail. The goal to kill people prevailed, but the goal to crush us, to crush our economy, to crush our belief in democracy, to crush our belief in our religions—that didn't work. People aren't crushed. If anything, they're stronger.

AND IF YOU GIVE YOURSELF TO THE HUNGRY

AND SATISFY THE DESIRE OF THE AFFLICTED,

THEN YOUR LIGHT WILL RISE IN DARKNESS

AND YOUR GLOOM WILL BECOME LIKE MIDDAY.

AND THE LORD WILL CONTINUALLY GUIDE YOU,

AND SATISFY YOUR DESIRE IN SCORCHED PLACES,

AND GIVE STRENGTH TO YOUR BONES;

AND YOU WILL BE LIKE A WATERED GARDEN,

AND LIKE A SPRING OF WATER WHOSE WATERS DO NOT FAIL.

THOSE FROM AMONG YOU WILL REBUILD THE ANCIENT RUINS;

YOU WILL RAISE UP THE AGE-OLD FOUNDATIONS;

AND YOU WILL BE CALLED THE REPAIRER OF THE BREACH,

THE RESTORER OF THE STREETS IN WHICH TO DWELL.

(ISAIAH 58:7–12)

*"It will never rain roses: when we want to have
more roses we must plant more trees."*

—*George Eliot*

*"Many of life's failures are experienced by people
who did not realize how close they were
to success when they gave up."*

—*Thomas Edison*

*"If you believe breaking is possible,
believe fixing is possible."*

—*Rabbi Nachman of Breslov*

CHAPTER 7

Principle No. 6:
Live Inspired

We never know which day will be our last. I'm confident that if we knew we only had twenty-four hours to live, we'd lead our lives differently than we're doing today. We'd live with a greater sense of urgency to do what's truly important in our lives. We know that our time is limited.

In reality, most of us don't live with such alacrity and awareness. We go about our daily routines without a care in the world. We wake up, get dressed, go to work, eat meals, socialize, and go to sleep. We repeat the ritual again and again. Life fast becomes a blur of one day blending into the next. I'd venture we all experience this phenomenon.

In a moment of crisis, we awaken to the fragility of life. We're motivated when we sense our mortality. Who wouldn't be? It's like the two-minute warning in a football game. I'm always amazed how much is accomplished, how much ball movement occurs, in the final seconds. The urgency drives a team to focus.

Ironically, the brush with mortality brings blessing.

One of the most moving poems I ever read, "Renascence" by Edna St. Vincent Millay, encapsulates this idea. The narrator complains that the world is so small, so restricting, and so filled with pain, suffering, and evil. She laments that there is no hunger she does not herself experience. Unable to cope with the pain, the poet begs God to take her from this world, and she soon finds herself lying peacefully in a grave. Here, a full six feet underground, she is finally free from the travails and pains of life.

Suddenly, the rain begins to fall and she hears raindrops pattering on her roof. She suddenly seems to love the sound far more than ever. She writes, "for rain it hath a friendly sound to one who's six feet underground." From her grave, the poet hopes she can once more see the rain and smell the fresh and fragrant breeze that wafts from the drenched and dripping apple trees:

> HOW CAN I BEAR IT, BURIED HERE,
>
> WHILE OVERHEAD THE SKY GROWS CLEAR
>
> AND BLUE AGAIN AFTER THE STORM?
>
> THAT I SHALL NEVER, NEVER SEE
>
> SPRING-SILVER, AUTUMN-GOLD . . .
>
> O GOD, I CRIED, GIVE ME NEW BIRTH,
>
> AND PUT ME BACK UPON THE EARTH!

Suddenly, a great thunderstorm strikes the grave and she senses a fragrance that only a living thing can sense. She exclaims, "I know not how such things can be; / I breathed my soul back into me." Jumping up from the ground she hugs the trees and proclaims:

OH GOD, I CRIED, NO DARK DISGUISE
CAN E'ER HEREAFTER HIDE FROM ME
THY RADIANT IDENTITY.
THOU CANST NOT MOVE ACROSS THE GRASS
BUT MY QUICK EYES WILL SEE THEE PASS,
NOR SPEAK, HOWEVER SILENTLY,
BUT MY HUSHED VOICE WILL ANSWER THEE . . .
GOD, I CAN PUSH THE GRASS APART
AND LAY MY FINGER ON THY HEART.

Edna St. Vincent Millay was only twenty years old when she wrote this most inspiring religious poem. For most of us, life-altering events generate an awakening. A baby is born, a couple is wed, someone close to us dies, we celebrate another milestone, or we survive a brush with death. However, life is not intended to be lived this way. Imagine how glorious our lives would be if we savored every moment.

Here's the reality: When we experience a brush with death, we become attuned to the simple gifts of life. Every breath becomes blessed. Recently, I experienced this sensation firsthand. I was jarred from life's routines. I had a kidney stone. People say it's more painful than childbirth. Of course, I don't know about that, but the pain was excruciating. It's hard to believe that one microscopic element can create so much havoc. We take the simplest activities for granted until they are disrupted.

How do you think I felt when the stone passed? Fantastic! I gained a renewed appreciation for a Jewish blessing. This may be hard to believe, but there's a blessing recited upon leaving the bathroom in expression of gratitude that every part of the body is working properly. We thank God that what is open is open and what is closed is closed. If there's a single blockage, we couldn't stand before him! When the kidney stone passed, I recited the blessing with renewed joy. Yet wouldn't it be wonderful if we sensed the blessings of a healthy body all the time? Even more so, how much happier would we be if we expressed gratitude even when our bodies faltered and in faith realized the miracle of life? This is how life is meant to be lived. God is everywhere. Do we open our eyes? We're meant to live with "radical amazement." Rabbi Abraham Joshua Heschel coined this phrase and challenged humanity: "Get up in the morning and look at the world in a way that takes nothing for granted. Everything is phenomenal, everything is incredible. Never treat life casually. To be spiritual is to be amazed." When we live in amazement, every moment is fresh and infused with infinite potential.

Deep down, we wish we could live every day as if it were our last. We want to live with urgency every day. We don't want to let our lives go by so quickly but want to live with deep joy and inspiration. How do we exude a sheer joy for the gift of life? How do we live with heightened spiritual sensitivity? How do we tune in to a greater frequency? How can we avoid wasting time so we are driven to greatness and experiencing God's glory? This chapter will guide you through the obstacles and opportunities of living inspired every day and guide you on how to be alert to the deep pleasures of everyday life. You will learn how to:

1. Tap into a higher frequency of living.
2. Discover divine design in your life.
3. Live in amazement.
4. Attune yourself to sacred moments every day.
5. Rise above the monotony of daily life.

Join me on a journey to live inspired!

Foundations

Inspiration flows when we harness the fullest potential of every moment. Living inspired means recognizing the inspiration in every flower or friend. How do we transform a mundane moment into one of radical amazement? How do we lead our lives on a higher frequency?

Life is not intended to be lived as a series of valleys and few peaks. God designed us with a soul sensory mechanism to live inspired every day. When I was growing up in Atlanta, we'd say, "I get high with a little help from Hashem (God)."

One of the great Greek philosophers, Marcus Aurelius, encapsulates this approach to life by stating, "When you arise in the morning, think of what a precious privilege it is to be alive—to breathe, to think, to enjoy and to love." Very little is needed to make us happy when we find a way to live in amazement. It's no wonder that in the Ethics of the Fathers, the classic treatise of wisdom, one of the forty-eight ways to gain wisdom is to be fascinated with life, to see life fresh and new every day!

The nature of humanity is to become habituated to the beauty and blessing around us and to become bored. The greatest proof of this phenomenon within humanity emerged at the beginning of time. We forget that Adam and Eve were commanded to eat from all of the trees of the Garden of Eden. God wanted them to enjoy all of the pleasures of the world. They could partake of anything—except for the fruit of one tree. Soon enough, they only desired the forbidden fruit.

How do we live inspired and infuse the mundane and monotonous with meaning? The etymology of the word "inspiration" offers a few clues. First, the literal sense of the word signifies the act of inhaling. To be inspired, we must slow down, breathe deeply, and focus on the present.

In his book *Time and the Art of Living*, Robert Grudin writes, "Because we believe that one moment is more or less like the next, we lose touch with the essential urgency of the present, the fact that each passing moment is the one moment for the practice of freedom." We possess a choice each moment to live or die, to grow or decay—in this instant and right now. We will never have this moment again. What will we do that will be worthy of future memory?

All too often, we're trapped by the past and mesmerized by the future. We lament the passing of time. Too often we spend our lives wondering, "What if?" or "If only . . ." By living in the past, we miss opportunities right in front of our eyes.

I'm sure we're all familiar with the following scenario. We approach the summer with anticipation. We relish the ten weeks of relaxation and think of all we want to accomplish. As the hot weather recedes in our rearview mirrors and Labor Day beckons, we all ask how the summer went by so fast. Where did the time go? This question is the challenge of life. Time waits for no one. It moves. Life happens in a blur.

Imagine that we're invited to a wedding. We all know the time will pass quickly, and before we know it, we'll be saying good-bye to family and friends. We'll likely regret not spending enough time with certain friends. When we arrive, we must be present. We must turn off our cell phones, Instagram, and Facebook and be present with the people around us. We must stay engaged in conversation with the person in front of us. When we do, we'll leave the wedding with a sense of time well spent in developing relationships and in the celebration.

Some of us live in the future. We're captivated by tomorrow. Zig Ziglar calls it "destination disease." Our happiness is conditional on a goal. We think, *When I retire, I'll be happy. When I get a raise, I'll be happy. When I go on vacation, I'll be happy. I can't wait until my children leave the house; then my wife and I will have time.* In reality, living inspired requires living in the present. We can't control what happens to us but only how we see the world around us. As Ralph Waldo Emerson wrote, "What lies behind you and what lies in front of you pales in comparison to what lies inside of you."

Happiness emerges from unlocking the potential in any moment and appreciating the gift of every breath. Ask someone with lung disease how much they yearn to breathe normally. The book of Genesis teaches that God created man by blowing his breath into humanity. Every breath we take is God's way of awakening within us the sacredness of every second. *Every moment is new; every breath is fresh and endowed with the potential for eternal resonance.*

Inspiration is everywhere when we stop and look. I call it the "burning bush" phenomenon. Redemption began in the Bible when Moses responded to the miracle of a bush that was on fire yet not consumed. He paused to reflect on the anomaly, unlike many who walked by without noticing. Moses was the only person who saw the bush afire and asked, "What is happening in front of me? What does it mean?" Living inspired requires gazing at the burning bushes in our midst and asking why they're there.

I'm forever grateful for pausing at a burning bush on a run in downtown Indianapolis. I looked forward to exploring the area on a beautiful night illuminated by a full moon and warmed by a soft breeze. As I ran past Bankers Life Fieldhouse, I approached an underpass below the interstate and noticed an array of cardboard boxes likely left by people seeking shelter. Then, out of the corner of my eye, as I ran under the bridge, I noticed a book neatly placed on one of the boxes. It was brand-new and entitled *40 Days to Lasting Change: An Aha Challenge* by Kyle Idleman. I picked up the book and opened it to a chapter called "Listen to the Wake-Up Calls in Your Life." Well, I then realized that somebody must've placed the book there in the hopes of inspiring a homeless person to find strength and hope. I was inspired by this deliberate act of kindness by an anonymous person. For me, the book was a burning bush.

The following morning, I ran back to the place and saw a city worker cleaning the area. The book was still there from the previous night. I asked him, "Were there homeless people here last night?" He replied, "Yeah, they come every night and I try to offer a kind word." I showed him the book and told him that he was engaged in holy work, like the mysterious book donor, to give the impoverished a sense of possibility and hope. The shining moon of the previous night, the book, and the street cleaner reawakened within me the knowledge that inspiration is everywhere when we stop, gaze, and wonder at the burning bushes in our lives.

Keep in mind the words of the poet Elizabeth Barrett Browning: "Earth's crammed with heaven, / And every common bush afire with God, / But only he who sees takes off his shoes; / The rest sit round and pluck blackberries." *The secret to living inspired is in knowing that though we can't stop time, we can slow it down by infusing fleeting moments with meaning; we can harness every moment for eternity.*

As a rabbi, one of the most stirring moments for me at a wedding is when I'm standing beneath the chuppah, the wedding canopy, awaiting the bride and groom. As they're escorted by their parents, I sense the fulfillment of dreams, love, and continuity. I think of my family and the joy and angst of separation as a parent lets go of a child. My heart is moved every time.

One time was notably different. As I was about to begin the ceremony, I began to cry uncontrollably. I learned before the wedding that the bride's mother had died at a young age. I couldn't help but think of my mother, of blessed memory, who had died more than twenty years ago and who had never met my wife, Diane, and our children. She wasn't there to walk me down the aisle. Rather than simply wipe away my tears and begin the service, I shared why I was crying. I opened up my heart to the young bride, Shoshana. I unlocked the moment and let out the stirring in my soul. I told her that although my mother was not physically present with me, I felt her presence the day I wed Diane in South Carolina. I assured Shoshana that just as I knew my mom was with me, her mother, Marsha, was with her, too. I think the entire room shed tears for my mother and for Marsha. They weren't tears of sadness but ones of comfort and joy.

Upon reflection, I realized my mother, who was a teacher, taught me a life-affirming lesson. It would've been easy for me as the officiating rabbi to try hiding my emotions. However, when I revealed a layer of my soul, I fueled my inner fire and ignited the souls of everyone in the room.

Living inspired means that any moment can be memorable and eternal. It depends on our mental presence and capacity to be in that moment. As Judaism teaches, any person can achieve a share in eternity in one hour, one moment. Rabbi Itamar Schwartz, a Jerusalem sage, reflected, "Every moment in which we do not live a sense of heightened awareness of the Divine within is not living."

You're likely reading this book because you do want to stop and cherish the gift of life, live in the moment, and harness the power of each day. You can and you will. As we continue through this chapter, I'll share stories and strategies that will enable you to achieve this goal and live life with enthusiasm and passion, but before I do, let's explore a second dimension to embodying this principle.

Living inspired emerges not only from being in the moment and appreciating the gift of the present but also in realizing a higher purpose in every encounter. Some moments are fleeting but others, the peak experiences, remain with us forever. How do we distinguish between the two?

At a recent conference on reverse engineering your life, Justin, a participant from Ocala, Florida, shared the difference between a peak moment and a temporal experience: "A peak moment gives you a revelation about the purpose of your life. A temporal experience gives you only the emotion of the moment."

The greatest pleasures in life emerge from discovering the meaning of every moment. When the stars align, we experience a deep joy and life affirmation. In the movie *Sleepless in Seattle*, who can forget the scene on the Empire State Building when Sam and Annie find each other? It's Heaven on Earth, for they realize that all of the twists and turns of fate led to their destiny.

Peak experiences happen when we're expressing not only who we are but who we want to be. Think about it for a moment. What gives us the deepest joy? Which pleasures are real and lasting and which are temporal? The measure of a life well lived reflects the nature of our investments. If our goal is simply to sample the finest foods, our stomachs may be full and our hunger nourished, but within hours we're hungry again, forget the experience, and are empty inside. However, when we feed others by sharing our bounty, the nourishment lasts forever. This pleasure generates inspiration and reflects our soul aspirations. It fills us with love, meaning, and significance.

The question of whether we allow time to pass by in a blur or maximize each moment depends on the kind of food we feed our souls. Do we pursue a purposeful life or one driven by pleasure? To live inspired is possible; to get high on life is optimal and infuses our lives with heightened significance and meaning.

How do we do it? By believing that *no day is without purpose and no moment is without meaning*. Realizing that today may be the only day we possess—this hour may be the one that can affect our lives forever—raises the stakes of time. How can we even think of killing time when each moment may not be a fleeting moment but eternal?

Every encounter is by divine design. We meet someone at work, someone holds the door for us, we receive a phone call asking for assistance, we exchange a glance. How many times have we heard people say that their life was changed because of a friendship, a kind word, or the growth achieved when forging ahead and moving outside their comfort zone?

There is the latent possibility that this moment may be sacred and worthy of memory. How will we know? How do we know when to engage and when to remain passive? What should we do to ensure we don't miss these moments? The answer is to be present and be engaged in life. Sometimes we experience uplifting moments when we least expect them. It all depends on whether we watch as events unfold before our eyes from the sidelines or whether we jump in and participate.

A number of years ago, one of our daughters, Michal, learned this lesson well. She was spending the year in Israel, and we encouraged her to take full advantage of the experience. After six months, she let us know that she more fully understood our advice. She shared the following story.

One afternoon, my friends and I were walking in the Malcha neighborhood in Jerusalem. As we crossed the street, we saw a parade of people celebrating the completion of a Torah scroll, the five books of Moses. It was a festive occasion with music and spirit. Counterintuitively, we joined the parade and walked in the procession. When we arrived at the synagogue, the new home of the Torah, the parade ended and we planned on resuming our neighborhood stroll. However, a woman approached us and said, "I am dedicating this Torah and we will not continue celebrating until you join us at the celebratory meal." We had no choice but to celebrate with her and her family. At the end of the festivities, the donor could not thank us enough for enhancing her event. She felt her father had sent us to make the day so special.

Michal added, "That was one of the most spontaneous moments of my life but one of the most meaningful." Inspiration flows when we harness the fullest potential of every opportunity and tap into a higher frequency. Michal could've walked by the parade and remained self-absorbed with her friends. Instead, she moved outside her comfort zone, took a risk, and seized the opportunity.

If we don't want to live with regret, we need to take a chance. In particular, when we have the opportunity to give to another, it's a call to transcend ourselves. We reminded Michal that the experience reinforced a message from a few years ago. As parents, we associate certain songs with each of our daughters. Michal's song is "I Hope You Dance," by Lee Ann Womack. The words reflect one of the strategies for living inspired: "When you get a choice to sit it out or dance, I hope you dance, I hope you dance." In Jerusalem, she chose to dance, and so can we. Do not be a spectator of life and sit it out. Participate and dance!

In my interview with Rolling Stone keyboardist Chuck Leavell, he described the sense of living in the groove: "Like the passage of time, music is marked by measure and beats, but when we make music swing, you get into the groove. The groove is everything. You can be a proficient music player, but if you're not in the groove, you're not playing music. I want my grandchildren to find their groove and make it as deep as can be. It is a moment of synergy when life is not marked by the passage of time but flows within itself."

Are we living in the groove?

In truth, we never know which instant of our lives will be the one we'll never forget. We tend to assume that the holiest moments occur when we plan for them, but often they occur when we least expect it, and in the oddest places. The biblical story of Jacob and the ladder, which we learned about earlier in the book, exemplifies this idea. He's running away from his brother, Esau, and he lies down to sleep on a dirty clod of earth. In the middle of the night, he has a dream from God assuring him of divine protection. He sees a ladder with angels ascending and descending. His proclamation upon awakening is one of the secrets of living inspired: "God is in this place and I did not know. This place is none other than the house of God and the gates to Heaven." When Jacob placed his head on the ground, he had no idea he'd be transformed. The ground was simply a place to rest. Yet he was astounded to discover that in this place, he experienced a divine vision. In this place, he touched eternity.

Whether we live inspired depends on our openness to these holy sparks. In my life, I've discovered such moments in the least likely places. One such experience occurred at JFK airport a few years ago. Until this day, when I walk in the area outside of security, I say to myself, "God was in this place and I did not know." The moment changed my life, my family's life, and hundreds of people's lives. I'm forever grateful that in that second, I wasn't checking my phone but was present to witness what transpired around me. Here's what happened: My second daughter Michal was on her way to study in Israel for her gap year. As we were getting ready to say good-bye, I struggled with the words to share with her. What would you say? "Don't forget to write, be safe, I love you?" In that moment, out of the corner of my eye, I saw a father place his hands on his daughter's head as he looked her in the eyes. He chanted some words that I intuitively knew to be the priestly blessing, the words in the book of Numbers: "May God watch over you, may God turn his face to you, may God shine on you and grant you peace."

God sent me a message. Those were the words I'd share with my daughter. I placed my hands on her head, looked into her eyes, and gave her the blessing. The words flowed from my heart into her heart.

What happened in the days ahead from that one moment transformed my life. It felt great to give her the blessing. As I was driving from the airport with our family, I contemplated giving this blessing to all of my daughters every Friday night. You might be wondering, *Why wouldn't you?* I wanted to give the blessing on Friday nights but I also didn't want to take away from my father's tradition. In some Jewish homes, the tradition is to offer the blessing weekly to one's children, but in our home the custom was to only give the blessing on the eve of the Day of Atonement, the holiest day of the year.

A couple of days later, I called my father in Israel and shared my dilemma. He responded with words I'll never forget: "If you have the opportunity to look your daughter in the eyes every week and give her a blessing, you definitely should." Then he added with the utmost humility, "If I had to do it all over again, I would've given you and your siblings a blessing each week."

I began giving blessings to our daughters every Friday night. Diane joins me as well. Over the years, we've given hundreds of blessings—*all generated by one moment of being mindful and present at JFK airport. God was in that place and I did not know.*

The story goes on and grows.

I shared my father's words on a Sabbath morning in Stamford. On the following Monday, I received the following e-mail from a friend, Maury Rosenbaum: "Rabbi, it's not too late for your father to start giving you a blessing." He was right. I called my dad in Israel and said, "I'm in my forties and you're in your seventies, but I'd love for you to start giving me a blessing." My father responded that he'd love to bless me. Now, years later, every Friday morning, I call my father in Israel. He shares his wishes for me over the phone, six thousand miles away and hours later, and we turn to our children and offer them a blessing as well.

I shudder when I contemplate the power of one moment in time—a few seconds at JFK airport—when I could've been oblivious to the sanctity of the place but instead, thank God, I was open to seeing the infinite and the rays of the divine in the terminal. The place was and is a gate to Heaven for me, my family, and thousands of people. I've shared this story in many seminars and, without a doubt, many people of all faiths have started the practice of blessing children and grandchildren, both in person and virtually—all due to one moment of living inspired.

One final thought. I don't know, nor likely ever will, the name of the person who blessed his daughter and inspired me. I can only imagine his encounter with God at the end of his life. God will evaluate his impact on the world, his joys, and disappointments. God will turn to the man and say, "Do you remember the day in August 2012 when your daughter was on her way to Israel and you gave her a blessing? You may not remember the moment, but someone was watching you. It was a rabbi from Connecticut who was inspired to bless his own children, whose father began blessing him, and now thousands of blessings were unleashed on the world all because of you!"

Little did he know the world was watching.

Imagine how different our lives would be if we were ready for the divine each hour of our lives. We wake up, thank God, and then proceed through a routine. We get dressed, eat, work, socialize, and go to sleep. We may read, watch TV, or surf social media. One hour runs into the next, one day into another, until time passes and life is a blur. Yet all around us and inside of us, we're changing and growing. The question is whether we notice, whether we pause, and whether we embrace the place. When we do, we'll live inspired every day!

Strategies

Live with Uncertainty: My Dad and Denzel Washington

My father and Denzel Washington both grew up in Mount Vernon, New York. Little did I know that they also share an abiding faith in God and a zest for living, rooted in an ever-present appreciation for the fragility of life. They both understand that living with uncertainty is a key to living inspired.

My father is one of the most grateful people I know. Whenever I ask him how he is doing, he responds, "Thank God!" with gusto. He sees every day with renewed mission and purpose. Recently, I asked him about how he stays "high" on life.

He responded with an insight from one of his mentors, Rabbi Moshe Besdin, whose wisdom shaped his outlook on life. When the biblical figure Jacob faced a reunion with his brother after many years of estrangement, he was anxious about the impending meeting and prepared simultaneously for peace and war. He prayed to God for assistance by saying, "I am diminished from all of my kindnesses." He acknowledged that he may no longer be deserving of God's grace and asked for God's mercy. My father explained that Jacob lived with uncertainty. He never believed that he was owed anything by God. When we live with a sense of healthy insecurity, we relish life's blessings. How can we not be filled with gratitude?

My father lives with this message. So does Denzel Washington. In an interview, the Academy Award–winning actor shared that he always carries a tattered notebook with him. He never wants to forget the list he maintained of job leads when he was looking for his first break in the business. In a recent speech, Denzel suggested, "Give thanks for blessings every day. Every day. Embrace gratitude. Encourage others. It is impossible to be grateful and hateful at the same time."

When Denzel concluded his speech, he ended with a prayer that he frequently uses when speaking to groups: "I pray that you put your slippers way under your bed at night so that when you wake up in the morning you have to start on your knees to find them. And while you are down there, say 'thank you.'"[12]

Living inspired stems from an awareness that life can change in an instant. Take nothing for granted. Don't assume you're owed anything. Don't live with a sense of entitlement. We're here by the grace of God.

> *"Life changes in the instant.*
> *The ordinary instant."*
>
> —Joan Didion, *The Year of Magical Thinking*

Tool Box

❶ **Carry a notebook.** What article do you possess that reminds you of your humble beginnings? Never forget the journey.

❷ **Write a letter of thanks to your parents, a mentor, or a friend for the foundations they laid for your success.**

❸ **Make a Joy List.** Write out the times you danced with joy. Identify the common denominator. Find ways to expand the list and ask others to describe their greatest joys.

Make Gratitude Great: The Daily Journal

No matter how stressful the day might be with six children running around and the pressure of rabbinical life, my mother always exhibited an optimistic outlook on life. Her spirit lives in me. Her attitude of gratitude is also ingrained within her namesake, my oldest daughter, Sara Malka, who taught me a valuable tool for living an inspired life. One day, as I was driving in Stamford, I called my home and Sara Malka answered the phone. She explained that she couldn't speak at the moment since she was on hold on the nationally syndicated *Dennis Prager Show*. Within minutes I heard the broadcaster on the radio in my car say, "Welcome, Sara from Connecticut." He asked callers to share the sources of happiness in their lives.

When asked about her secret to maintaining gratitude, she shared that every night she recorded an expression of gratitude in a journal. I had no idea about her holy habit. To her credit, she doesn't say at the end of every day, "Thank God, I am alive," and the next day, "Thank God, I am alive," and so on, but she finds a new source of joy to share every day. At the time of the call, she had accumulated 770 entries. Wow! Most important, she reviews fifty of them every night to foster her sense of gratitude.

What are you waiting for? Start today. Leading an inspired life requires a disciplined approach to cultivating an appreciation for God's gifts. All we need to do is stop, reflect, and write.

Tool Box

❶ **Start a gratitude journal today.** Write in it every day. Don't repeat the same thing over and over. Review your list every day. Count your blessings.

❷ **Participate in the fifteen-minute exercise "Mental Subtraction of Positive Events"** (available at *http://ggia .berkeley.edu/practice/mental_subtraction_positive_events*). Consider the ways in which positive events in your life might never have taken place and reflect on what life would be like without them. (Watch *It's a Wonderful Life* for inspiration.)

❸ **Write a letter of gratitude to a friend or relative who has always supported and inspired you.**

Seeing Serendipity

Do we see serendipity? It's a key to living inspired. A friend recently shared:

> Rabbi, I have to tell you what happened. I sensed divine providence. I was at a conference for the banking industry. As you know, my expertise lies in a unique area concerning insurance benefits, and I know people need my services, but I have trouble finding clients. God was watching over me. At the hotel registration desk, there was a fellow from a national bank who was also checking in at the same time. I introduced myself and we struck up a conversation. It turned out when I asked him what he did, he responded that he was in charge of the national insurance trusts for which I was best suited. We spoke in the lobby for about an hour, and he told me that he was struggling with the answer to a challenging problem in his world, and I was his answer. I couldn't believe my good fortune.

One encounter, seemingly random but, in truth, by divine design.

Most of us don't pause to appreciate serendipity in our lives. We move from one day to the next, one meeting to another, without exploring the connections between them. How did this person come into my life? How would my life be different if I'd been born in a different place? We're stuck in traffic and come late to an event or even miss it. How do we respond?

Only in hindsight do we often realize the benefit of a sudden change in our plans. Growing up, I learned the motto, "This, too, is for the best." This doesn't mean that we rely solely on a higher power. We must do our best to participate in our future, but when all is said and done, when we live with the faith that a higher power runs the world, we gain a new perspective and a deeper faith. We're inspired by serendipity in our lives.

Tool Box

Here are some steps to cultivate an awareness of the hidden and holy.

❶ **Describe an out-of-the-ordinary event in your life.** What led to it?

❷ **Describe an experience when initial disappointment was transformed by hindsight into gratitude.** How did your understanding of the event change? Why?

❸ **Identify three significant events in your life and trace the path to their fruition.** Were the events by chance or design?

❹ **Identify three people who've made a difference in your life.** How did you meet them? By chance or design?

❺ **Share an experience where you saw God's hand in your life.** Ask a friend to share their experience.

Twelve Seconds to a Better You

What are the first words you exclaim when you wake up in the morning? Do you hit snooze or do you realize that you're blessed today with eighteen hours to seize life, grow, serve, and develop into your best? Judaism teaches that the gift of speech separates us from the animal kingdom and enables us to emulate God. The very first words uttered by God in the Bible were "Let there be light!" Our tradition teaches that the very first words upon rising in the morning should be, "Thank God, I'm alive!" When we wake up and say these simple words, we reorient our perspective on the day ahead. In fact, Judaism recommends a twelve-word formula as a tool for living inspired.

God works in mysterious ways. The following likely apocryphal story illuminates the secret of the twelve-second formula. At a United States convention for neurologists from all over the world, one of the main topics was the phenomenon of people who fainted upon getting up from bed after waking. One of the speakers was Professor Linda McMaron of Great Britain, and she gave a lengthy speech regarding her study on this issue. She shared that after many years of study and investigation, she had come to the conclusion that the fainting was caused by the sharp transfer between lying down and standing up. She said that it takes twelve seconds for the blood to flow from the feet to the brain. But when a person quickly stands up after waking, the blood gets "thrown" into the brain too quickly, resulting in fainting for some people. This phenomenon is known as orthostatic hypotension. She suggested that everyone, even those who didn't have a tendency to faint upon waking, should sit on the edge of the bed and slowly count to twelve before getting up, to avoid dizziness, weakness, and/or fainting. Her speech was rewarded with loud applause and enthusiastic feedback.

Another professor, a Jewish man, asked permission to speak. He said, "In our tradition, we recite a prayer of thanks to the Creator of the World for meriting us to wake up healthy and whole. The prayer is said immediately upon waking up, while one is still on the bed and sitting down. There are twelve words in this prayer, and if one regulates himself to say it slowly with concentration, it takes exactly twelve seconds to say it . . . twelve words in twelve seconds."

He then said the prayer slowly in Hebrew: *Mode Ani Lefanecha*

Melech Chai Vekayam, Shehechezarta Bi Nishmati Bechemla Raba Emunatecha. (I give thanks to You, Source of life and existence, that you have once again placed my soul within me: great is your faith in me.) The audience burst into a standing applause that roared throughout the auditorium. This time, it was for the Creator of the World.

Regardless of your faith tradition, imagine the impact, upon rising from sleep, of a twelve-second declaration of faith in the Almighty and an expression of thanksgiving. We'll not only feel grateful for being alive but we'll greet the day with a renewed sense of divine purpose and appreciation of life.

Formulate your own morning message, pledge twelve seconds to a better you, and capture the spirit of gratitude every day!

Tool Box

❶ **Recite the Modeh Ani, the twelve-second formula, in the morning:** "I give thanks to You, Source of life and existence, that you have once again placed my soul within me: great is your faith in me."

❷ **Pray, meditate, and seize the day upon awakening.**

❸ **Bless every gift:** Open your eyes, stretch your hands, walk on your feet, breathe deeply.

One more thought about living inspired and tuning in to a higher frequency: Life is not about counting the days but making each day count. Remember 168. It represents the hours in a week. We don't remember the days but the hours. Each hour is a window to eternity.

Each hour can be one of spiritual power. Time passes quickly unless we slow it down.

When I conduct a funeral, I almost always highlight the fact that there will never be another moment as this one right now—this exact constellation of people from all walks of life paying tribute to one person. We're all at the service for a purpose. When we leave, we can go back to living our lives as if nothing has changed or we can grow from the experience. What can we learn from the life we mourned and celebrated at the memorial service? Recently, I shared about a woman who always put other people first. What will be said about us? Living inspired means taking those words to heart, understanding that we're meant to hear those words today and we must do our best to rededicate ourselves to "putting other people first."

Imagine the day after the funeral. We walk into the office on a Monday morning. Our e-mail in-box is full, we're swamped with work, and then we receive a phone call from a friend who needs our wisdom or support; it's a timely issue. Rather than ignore the call, we remember the inspiration from yesterday. We think about "putting other people first" and make an extra effort to carve out a window of time to give the person the strength they need. Years later, we discover that our words were just what our friend needed to hear on that day and gave him or her the emotional strength to make one of the most important decisions of their life. It changed their destiny. How did it all happen? By remembering and heeding the words we heard at a funeral on Sunday. The words didn't go in one ear and out the other but penetrated our hearts.

All we have is today. Yesterday is gone and tomorrow is yet to come. This one day, the moment you're now experiencing, is holy. Unlock it. Cherish it. Harness its full potential. When we live inspired, we can slow down the clock and create enduring memories, enrich friendships, and deepen our impact. We can lead lives of legacy!

Celebrity Stirrings

Ron Howard, the American film director, producer, and actor, exudes a joy for life. From playing Opie Taylor in the sitcom *The Andy Griffith Show* to Richie Cunningham on *Happy Days*, his television persona of innocence, humor, optimism, and authenticity reflects his real-life personality. As mentioned earlier, he made a successful transition from actor to director, and his films, such as *Cocoon, Apollo 13, A Beautiful Mind*, and *In the Heart of the Sea* (just to name a few), embody the effervescence of the human spirit.

When I interviewed Ron, the principle of living inspired clearly came to the fore. His recollections serve as guideposts for everyone on a journey to lead a life of legacy. He shared about seeing beauty:

> One of the things that I like about my job is that I see things as stories, so I tend to parse out almost everything that I experience and make it into a beginning, middle, and an end. I just naturally start to do that. And the other thing is, over the years, even though I began as an actor, I've become much more visually sensitive. That's a great gift. That's a great blessing because I can look over and see the sun catching an object, leaves. At a certain moment I say, "Wow, that's a great image." I'll get these little snapshots, these compositions in my mind, and it's this constant reminder that nature, the world around us, is constantly providing us with powerful images that can pique our curiosity, satisfy our aesthetic sense of things, and inspire us, and make us grateful to be a part of the environment, nature.

One of the phrases Ron shared was "Never miss an opportunity to celebrate!" He spoke about a guy on his production sets who lives by this motto, and about inspiration from his wife, Cheryl, and his mom:

> In the middle of working on movies that are unbelievably arduous, often stressful, filled with people at their best but often at their worst, just raw emotions, there is a feeling like you're on a long voyage or an arduous expedition. This guy is great. He'll turn and say, "My friend Dave always says, 'Never miss a chance to celebrate.'" Anytime something good happens in the film, that's a reminder. A lot of wonderful things happen. Smell the roses; never miss an opportunity to celebrate.
>
> My wife, Cheryl, and I are both very good at bringing to our life a sense of gratitude, which we inherited from our parents separately, that reminds us to take pride in what we achieve and enjoy the benefits of what we've been able to earn, but also be grateful for those moments. There are a lot of them. Sometimes, it's just a great morning.
>
> My mom, Jean Howard, thoroughly believed in the power of positive thinking. Without being naive or overly simplistic, life did amaze her. Christmas was her favorite thing, and every Christmas was the best Christmas ever. Each one somehow, in her mind, surpassed any previous Christmas. Not all of her hopes and dreams were fulfilled. She had health problems. And she was honest about these things. But somehow she just exuded an appreciation and a joy for life.

The role of his mother in shaping his worldview especially struck a chord with me because of the influence of my own mother. The benefits of living inspired, seeing the beauty and splendor in life, affect not only us but our families and those around us. Life is filled with challenges. We'll always experience setbacks, and the rays of light may be blocked by clouds. Yet if we muster the ability to focus on the positive and celebrate the gifts, we'll lead our lives with joy. Every day won't be a blur but a blessing. We'll see every hour as fresh and filled with renewed possibility and purpose. Our lives will be enriched and inspired!

‖‖

CHAPTER 8

Principle No. 7: Discover Your Renewable Energy

You're on the most important journey of your life. It's more significant than any road trip, cruise, or career because this journey is about the real you—who you are and who you want to be through the span of your entire life.

You're reading this book because you truly want to be your best self and lead the life of your dreams. You want to make the most of every day and ensure that your actions reflect the essence of who you want to be. Most people start down the path of renewal, but within days they get stuck, only to look back months or years down the road and wonder what happened to all of their best intentions.

Here's the good news—that doesn't have to be you. You actually have an inborn, ever-ready energy pack designed to motivate you, inspire you, and direct you to leading the life you want to lead every day. The problem is that most of us are not aware of this gift inside of us. We neglect it. This final principle, discovering your renewable energy, will help you find that latent source of unbridled spiritual power inside of you. It's there from birth just waiting for you to draw on its infinite potential every day. It provides the source of your courage, strength, spirit, and sense of a higher purpose in life.

The Talmud teaches that an unborn child is taught the secrets of creation and knowledge in order to reach spiritual perfection. However, as the child is born, an angel strikes the baby above the mouth and he forgets these truths, and is born an unlearned baby. Why? What was the purpose of being taught the secrets if they would be forgotten upon birth?

Rabbi Joseph Soloveitchik suggests an answer that underscores a secret of the soul. The road to perfection is not forgotten but is buried deep within. Our souls possess the spiritual DNA for our life success and fulfillment. A lifetime of effort and soulful living will realize our divine potential. Why are the secrets buried in our souls? True pleasure emerges when we expend the effort to discover our potential. When we invest in our potential, when we bring our innate wisdom to reality, our souls sing. In the words of Rumi, "When you do things from your soul, you feel a river moving in you, a joy."

Discovering your renewable energy begins with the "Michelangelo principle." Michelangelo's sculpture *David* is one of the most famous statues ever created. It was unique and original in its time. Previous statues by sculptors Donatello and Verrocchio depicted David as a fierce warrior, holding the giant head of Goliath like a trophy. But Michelangelo's pose was almost relaxed or nonchalant, with a rock held loosely in his right hand and the slingshot slung casually over his shoulder. Yet his face calmly exudes the focused concentration of the vanquishing hero.

Michelangelo, a Renaissance painter, sculptor, architect, poet, and engineer, had amazing vision. He saw art where others only saw rock. He is quoted as saying, "In every block of marble I see a statue as plain as though it stood before me, shaped and perfect in attitude and action. I have only to hew away the rough walls that imprison the lovely apparition to reveal it to the other eyes as mine see it."

That's how God sees us. Just as the artist can see the art inside the block of stone, God can see the potential inside of us. He can find beauty beneath the rock. We only see this block of unfinished person. We sometimes don't see how to chisel away the heavy rock hiding our beauty. We're weighed down by the pressures that keep us confined, frozen in stone. God sees the graceful beauty, the influence, and the artwork inside of us. "Every block of stone has a statue inside it, and it is the task of the sculptor to discover it," Michelangelo said. "I saw the angel in the marble and carved until I set him free," Michelangelo said about one of his creations. It's the same for us. At the hands of the Master Sculptor, we can rise out of the rock, free to become the masterpiece he already sees within.

Reverse engineering your life is a lifelong approach to developing your potential and making your mark on the world. When you follow the steps to becoming your best self, you've only just begun. Whether it's daily, weekly, or monthly, the process of personal growth never stops.

Ron Howard shared with me, "Beyond my professional career in film, I think a lot about my civic responsibilities and social responsibilities. I try to organize my life without retiring and without ignoring my family."

My father embodies this message and serves as an inspiring role model for me. As a career educator, he spent many years as a principal in Atlanta, but after my mother died, he moved from one new position to another over a ten-year period. He had little job stability, yet he never got down. He'd always tell me that it must be that God had a new plan in store for him. He taught me that contrary to popular opinion, there is no such thing as retirement; we just have new missions and new opportunities.

In fact, when he formally retired as a high school principal, he reinvented himself upon moving to Israel. He blogs (see "Kosher Movies" at *www.koshermovies.com*), he teaches in a high school for Americans, he studies; he's launching a movie review cable series, exercises, and is truly doing his best to accomplish and discover new ways to impact the world.

He lives with the words of his mentor, Rabbi Aharon Lichtenstein, who wrote, "The significance of having aspirations and dreams is critical. We do not subscribe to the conception that it is better to have minimal aspirations so as to have maximal contentment. The moral life, the spiritual life, the religious life, is one of yearning and aspiration."

We never retire from life. *Retirement is an illusion.* If you're alive today, it's for a purpose. You may change your job, collect Social Security, or not be working outside the home, but you can always make a difference. This concept is the secret to discovering your renewable energy every day of your life.

The first step is in knowing and believing in the innate, latent potential inside of you. Your reading this book today signifies that you're destined to accomplish something important, impactful, and eternal. Your task in life is not simply to survive but to thrive. When I wake up in the morning, I not only declare my belief in God but God's belief in me. I'm here for a reason and so are you. We can and should make every day a masterpiece worthy of future memory.

Imagine for a minute that our greatest leaders followed the mandatory age of retirement. The world would be radically different. If Moses went to Florida at age sixty-five and spent his life finding early-bird specials and playing golf, how different the world would be! Moses and Aaron didn't start their careers until they were eighty and eighty-three, respectively. Abraham set out on his journey to promote ethical monotheism in his seventies. "Forty is the old age of youth," Victor Hugo once wrote, but "fifty is the youth of old age."

What gave them the strength to not sit back and enjoy their golden years? I think about my grandmother, who recently passed away at the age of 101. Until her last few years when she became ill, she sought to love, laugh, offer wisdom and her honest opinions, and made the most of every day. What motivates a person to seize the day for impact?

The answer is the secret to discovering your renewable energy. Every day God invests the world anew with life. Each day possesses a fresh breath and so do we. If we wake up in the morning, we're called upon to find meaning and purpose in that day. If we believe that we're endowed with a mission every day, then we realize the latent potential for holiness and eternity within the day. We see the world not for its problems but its possibilities.

As you're embarking on the journey to reverse engineer your life, you'll inevitably encounter resistance, both internal and external. You'll get distracted by the pace of life. You'll get pushed back by the pressures from your job, peers, and others. Internally, it's easier not to change and just revert to the status quo.

It's tough when we start a new project. It's like a diet. For the first day or two, we're really disciplined. Then life gets in the way. We go to a ball game, a wedding, or just eat too much. Then we have a choice. Do we give up or get back on the plan?

Life is too valuable to throw up your hands and say, "I can't!" This chapter will help you find the strength to say, "I can!" The process of reverse engineering your life is a lifelong investment in yourself. I guarantee you'll stumble from time to time. We all do. This chapter will help you get back on track and develop the habits and attitude to keep your dreams alive and embody them every day.

The principle of discovering your renewable energy will underscore how your ongoing investment will yield rewards beyond your dreams. The essence of this final step is developing the strength of spirit to stay true to your mission by cultivating a higher purpose. We'll explore how you can find the renewable energy to evaluate and elevate your life. The timeless wisdom, life experiences, and hands-on techniques given here will enable you to discover the fortitude to continually process the steps of reverse engineering your life while concurrently experiencing the enduring pleasure of living a life of purpose and perpetuity.

In this chapter you'll learn how to:

1. Become attuned to the real you.
2. Explore the anatomy of your soul.
3. Harness your source of renewable energy.
4. Learn strategies to access your inner power and potential.

Living a life of purpose means knowing that your actions reflect the real you—the gap between who you aspire to be and who you are gets smaller through alignment of your body and soul. There is no more bifurcation. As your new self unfolds, you'll begin to notice everything a little bit more, appreciate it, and embrace the chance to wake up and continue your road to personal growth and greatness.

Foundations

Who are you?

The answer to this question reflects whether you truly understand the difference between your mission and purpose. *Your mission is what you do. Your purpose is why you do it.* Your mission creates focus. Your purpose drives your passion. When we lead a life of purpose, we'll discover infinite capacity for renewal and growth.

Let's look at the world of business. What's the difference between a company's mission statement and its purpose? In 1960, in a speech by David Packard to Hewlett-Packard's training group, he said:

> I want to discuss why a company exists in the first place. In other words, why are we here? I think many people assume, wrongly, that a company exists simply to make money. While this is an important result of a company's existence, we have to go deeper and find the real reasons for our being.
>
> Purpose (which should last at least a hundred years) should not be confused with specific goals or business strategies (which should change many times in a hundred years). Whereas you might achieve a goal or complete a strategy, you cannot fulfill a purpose; it's like a guiding star on the horizon—forever pursued but never reached. Yet although purpose itself does not change, it does inspire change. The very fact that purpose can never be fully realized means that an organization can never stop stimulating change and progress.

The same idea applies even more so to our lives. Your mission or goal in life may change depending upon your age, family situation, career, and aspiration, but your life purpose transcends any one mission.

What do you live for? What drives you?

Listen carefully to an eternal truth: If your life is motivated by the size of your bank account or the largesse of your home, you'll never be satisfied. The wisest man of all time, King Solomon, reflected in Ecclesiastes, "A person who loves money will never have enough money." If your goal is honor and fame, you'll never ultimately be full.

Rediscovering your life purpose is more relevant now than ever. People are living longer these days. However, most of the world sees the challenge of a longer life in terms of a retirement nest egg. Will I have enough money for the added years? But the larger challenge is whether we make the most of our additional time. How do we enrich these additional years?

A recent study by the Rand Corporation reveals that a sizable segment of the population retires for a year or two with the intention of returning to the workforce. As John F. Kennedy stated in his conference on aging in 1963, "We have added years to life and now it is time to add life to those years."

I recently learned of the Halftime Institute, which blends precepts of Christian faith with ideas from management gurus like Peter Drucker and Jim Collins. It was designed to help individuals navigate the passage "from success to significance." Among other things, the Halftime Institute's programs help members find their calling through developing "a personal plan for spiritual growth, a life mission statement, and a clear action plan."

Lest you think I'm only writing this for ages sixty-five and up, I'm not. In truth, we're all faced with transitions, changes, and pauses in our careers, and we may experience setbacks. Though we can't always avoid these situations, we can control how we face these new possibilities. Do we retreat and lament our misfortune or do we seize our new scenario as a chance to forge a new frontier?

When we live with a higher purpose and aren't simply focused on the task and mission at hand, we can adapt to new scenarios and circumstances with passion and energy. In reality, if our purpose in life is beyond ourselves and ignites the lives of other people, there are multidimensional ways to spread light.

What do you do?

Most people answer this by responding with their profession: "I'm an actor, a doctor, a lawyer, a social worker, a homemaker," and so on. In truth, this answer reflects only one aspect of ourselves. Your profession is what you do, but it's not who you are. You may be an accountant and crunch numbers, or a teacher who's educating children, but this doesn't necessarily reflect your purpose in life. It's your mission at this moment to be a successful editor, but it's not your purpose.

We are not defined by what we do but by who we are and what we want to be. Unfortunately, when we confuse our mission with our purpose, if a time comes when we may no longer be able to perform our mission, need to change careers, or our life situation alters, we may be thrown for a loop. All of our attention has been devoted to building up our careers and other people's perception of us, and then when it's busted, we're awakened to the essence of who we really are and what gives us deep joy and pleasure in life. The following stories illustrate this idea.

Daren is a thirty-eight-year-old Los Angeles man dying from a degenerative nerve disease. Two years ago Daren was handsome, successful, and vibrantly healthy. He'd reached the pinnacle of professional success. He was a singer, dancer, and virtuoso guitarist, and was greatly sought after by many of the major Hollywood studios. He had a wife and two children, a lovely home, and ran five miles a day.

Today Daren is strapped to a wheelchair, unable to support his own body's weight. His lungs are so weak that he must consciously draw in enough air to make his vocal cords work. He can no longer move his arms, legs, or body. He needs help to go to the bathroom. His flesh is slowly melting away from his bones.

At first Daren was in agony because he couldn't play, couldn't dance, couldn't earn money, couldn't drive his new Mercedes, couldn't make love—in short, he could no longer live up to his models of who he thought he should be. But after time, he began to see that it wasn't his illness that was the problem.

"It was those damn models," he realized. "Those models were always a hassle for me. They're like balloons with holes in them. I've had to keep puffing and puffing all the time to keep them from collapsing. They're not really who I am." And gradually he's been able to let go of his identification with his models.

One day he said, "You know, I've never felt so alive in my whole life. I can see now how all the things I used to do to 'be somebody' actually separated me from really being alive. For all my outward success, my life back then was just a sort of busy, numb dullness."

He laughed and shook his head. "We're such fools, aren't we? We spend so much time polishing our personalities, strengthening our bodies, keeping up our social positions, trying to achieve this and that. We make such serious business of it all. But now that I can no longer do the things I thought were so important, I have so much love for so many things. I'm discovering a place inside I'd never looked at, never knew. None of the praise I received in the world brought me half the satisfaction I experience right now from just being."

Daren was stripped to his core and his essence. He realized that most of his life he was filling up his body rather than his soul. In the words of Gilda Radner, "While we have the gift of life, it seems to me that the only tragedy is to allow part of us to die—whether it is our spirit, our creativity, or our glorious uniqueness." Frequently, the litmus test is whether people admire us for what we possess or for who we are.

A number of years ago, I was visiting Los Angeles and stayed at a hotel opposite a well-known talent agency. Early Saturday morning, I glanced out the window and saw a stunning sports car pull up in the driveway of a towering glass building with camera and lights in tow. Flashbulbs popped as the driver, presumably a movie star, exited the car. But then something odd happened. After the car was empty, the cameras resumed taking photos of the car. I realized that the media frenzy when the car arrived had nothing to do with the person inside it but rather with his trappings.

In our society, we focus much honor on the external accoutrements but overlook the person inside. Who do we honor and what do we value in other people? What about our own self-perception? Do we lead our lives in a way that nourishes our best self or are we focused on feeding the misperceptions of others?

In her book *One-Minute Jewish Stories*, Shari Lewis illustrates how we all yearn to be loved for our true selves. Once upon a time, there lived a very poor couple who had a son. When the boy was born, a relative sent some expensive and elegant clothing as a present. The mother made a beautiful robe from the cloth and said, "When my son is a man, I'll send him into the world with this beautiful robe."

The boy grew up and one day a rich merchant invited all the townspeople to a feast. The son came in his usual tattered clothing and no one made room for him at the table. Brokenhearted at the rejection, he went home and told his mother what had happened. To console him, she gave him the beautiful robe that she had made from the elegant cloth, which had been stored away all these years.

The son returned to the feast dressed in his new finery. The rich man saw him, rushed over, and bowed, and asked him to sit beside him. The son took off his elegant robe, held it over the food, and said, "Eat robe, eat all you want."

"Why are you talking to your coat?" asked the rich man. "Because when I was here before in poor clothing," the boy replied, "no one paid attention to me. But now I come in a fancy robe and you treat me royally. It is clearly not me you invited to eat beside you, but my robe."

The lesson of this story is clear: If you love me for my robe, you rob me of myself. And, of course, the opposite is also true. If you love me for myself, you give me a treasure beyond price.

Transitions are hard in and of themselves but even more difficult when a person's life is so intertwined with a profession. This phenomenon is particularly notable in the area of sports.

In October 1993, at the age of thirty, Michael Jordan had already won three straight NBA titles, three straight NBA Finals MVP awards, and seven straight NBA scoring titles. Then, on October 5, 1993, the shocking words crossed the wire: "Michael Jordan will announce that he is retiring tomorrow at a press conference in Deerfield, Illinois." But did you know that Michael Jordan retired multiple times from basketball because his identity was so tied to his career?

Many athletes struggle with their role in life and the next steps after retiring from sports. They feel angst because their best days seem to be behind them. They live in the glories of years gone by. They bask in the aura of a winning shot, touchdown, or home run.

Yet contrast their retirement with that of Mariano Rivera, the greatest closer baseball has ever seen. He served as the anchor reliever of a nearly two-decade Yankees dynasty. For seventeen years, he was the closer, the go-to man who arrived in the ninth inning to protect a tight lead. In his final season, he pitched as well as he ever did. When people cite his greatness, they credit his natural athleticism and simplicity of his mechanics. All are true, but when asked himself, he acknowledges these traits with gratitude but believes that his greatness has no earthly source.

Upon his retirement from the big leagues, he embarked on a new mission in life. In an interview in *New York Magazine* he shared his vision of the essence of his persona and his success. It laid the groundwork for his renewable energy and sense of life purpose: "Everything I have and everything I became is because of the strength of the Lord, and through him I have accomplished everything. Not because of my strength. Only by his love, his mercy, and his strength. You don't own your gifts like a pair of jeans. My cutter does not belong to me. He could give it to anyone he wants, but you know what? He put it in me. He put it in me, for me to use it. To bring glory, not to Mariano Rivera, but to the Lord."[13]

> *"Live for yourself and you will live in vain.*
> *Live for another and you*
> *will live again."*
>
> —Bob Marley

Think of yourself as a flame. Your role in life is to ignite the flames of others. In the process, your light will not be diminished but the world will be much brighter!

Who is the real you? Knowing the answer to this question will likely determine your success in leading the life now for how you want to be remembered. More important, exploring the deeper meaning of these questions will fortify you to deepen your life purpose, enrich your relationships, seize every moment, and lead your life with urgency and passion.

Let's go deeper into the anatomy of your inner spark, soul, and the higher power within you, me, and everyone. Are you a body or something more? Are you a conduit for God or for your personal glory?

Hopefully, the process of reverse engineering your life has awakened within you a higher consciousness of the real you. You have inevitably sensed your divine spark, the quest for meaning, love, and purpose.

This chapter is geared toward helping you understand the anatomy of your soul. How does it work? How do you derive power from within? How do you draw strength and renewed energy from it every day of your life?

Before we begin, let's step back to the very beginning. We started this book with a vision of how we want to be remembered when we're gone. We harnessed the confrontation with our mortality to reignite a vision for our lives. We'll now reflect on the process of birth, the early days of our lives.

> *"Create in me a pure heart, O God, and*
> *renew a steadfast spirit within me."*
>
> —Psalm 51:1

Your body is finite and your soul is infinite. You're not merely flesh and bones. You're holy. You're a divine spark. You're unique.

You can and will make an indelible impact on another person every waking hour.

The human soul is indestructible and eternal. The Zohar (mystic Jewish literature on Kabbalah) teaches that energy never ceases to exist. "Nothing is lost in this world, even the breath of the mouth, even the word spoken by a human being, even a sound; all have their area and location. When someone stands between two mountains and emits a sound, the wind carries his voice to the mountains and returns it in the form of an echo. Through our actions, we enhance or debase this energy. Every action, spoken word, and meditation remains in existence and should inform the course of our lives. Our life choices lead to shame or glory, disgrace or eternal life."

We began our journey with the following statement: you are born with a purpose. Your mission in life transcends the particular circumstances, job, economic state, age, or state of health. As long as you breathe the air, you're renewed by God for a higher calling every day. Today, you begin your mission anew. What happened in the past is over and tomorrow is yet to come. Today is a world alone. You only possess this moment and this hour.

Your body gets tired, but your soul is inspired. I discovered the secret to finding wellsprings of strength in life. We're born into the world with our hands closed. When we die, our hands are open. Clench your hands. Close them. Slowly open them and unfurl your fingers. You've moved from self to soul, closed to open. This idea symbolizes our journey through life, and understanding this principle reveals the secret to unlocking your renewable energy.

A baby begins life as a recipient. Whether through parents, doctors, nurses, or the care of others, a newborn is dependent on others to live. A baby can only survive with the help of other people. The essence of life is learning how to develop from being a taker to being a giver. No matter who you are, no matter your race, age, creed, or faith, you were born as a baby—a small body and a pulsating spark.

Through life, we learn how to give and move from being self-centered to other-centered. We're not here for our own glory but for the glory of God and humankind. It's every person's mission to spread his or her light. The deeper we live this truth, the happier and more alive we'll be every day, and the more energized we'll be to embrace and pursue a life of purpose.

Listen carefully to the last will and testament of Rabbi Yechiel Michel Tucazinsky, a holy mystic and sage, to his family. His message echoes to all of us who desire an eternal life now and forever:

> This rule should be studied, never to be forgotten: Life has to have a purpose. Now if one calculates his "balance" for every business and also keeps account of his total outcome, he should certainly do the same with respect to life itself. Every year, every week, every day, every hour has its own balance sheet. Each and every one should never forget that finally, even if he should live for 120 years, he will be called to render a final accounting for all of his deeds and utterances.
>
> Furthermore, all man's deeds, devices, and output of energy are indestructible. If these are materialistic, they will be reduced to their material like bodily movements, sounds, the panting of animals and beasts. But if the actions, words, and thoughts are purposeful, they will ascend and raise their authors to the supernal and blissful worlds.
>
> May my descendants accustom themselves to remember that life has a purpose and a goal. If life is not directed toward some purpose, it flits like dust that flies away and a dream that dissipates without leaving behind anything of consequence. Life is a valuable possession and it would be a pity were it to be utterly lost.[14]

The question for us is whether we realize this verity now or wait until our assumptions are shaken and disturbed. We are vessels. We receive infinite potential when we're born into this world. We're seeds that are ready to grow. The source of our life fulfillment is the extent to which we nurture these seeds. I'll tell you why.

The deepest joys we experience in this world are when we sense that our lives have purpose and meaning. This book is ultimately about enabling you to lead a life filled with pleasure. When you lead a life of legacy, blessings well up inside of you. You're energized and inspired. Authentic happiness and motivation emerges from leading a life of purpose.

The more in tune you are with the real you, the soulful dimension of your personality, the better equipped you'll be to draw on that reservoir of strength and renewable energy. If you define yourself by your body, you'll get tired. If you define yourself by your soul, you'll shine.

There's a man in his midtwenties who seems to always be on fire. His name is Dovi and he has Williams syndrome. However, in spite of his seeming limitations, he is one of the most positive and upbeat people I know. He is optimistic, greets everyone with a smile, and lights up a room. He rarely passes anyone without asking them how they're doing. Recently, we honored him at our annual dinner with the Chai (Life) Award. I shared the following about him as I presented him with his award:

> If there is anyone in our community who cherishes life and brings joy to all he meets, it's our friend Dovi. One of the testaments to a holy person is whether his inside is like his outside. Dovi was born with a holy soul and sparks that smile every day. We all are, but Dovi lets his shine. From

the very beginning of his life, he's been upbeat, smiles, gives, and looks at how to make people happy. He embodies the essence of joy inside and out. I conducted a Dovi interview that I want to share with you. I asked Dovi, "What do you love about shul?" He said, "I love talking to people, greeting them." You can always find Dovi on Shabbat morning chatting with the officer. "What makes you happy?" Dovi answered, "Jewish singers, Leepa, Avraham's friend, his sister, brothers, going out with people, especially bowling and ice cream and making people happy."

Dovi loves life, loves people, and loves God. He loves getting called to the Torah and loves to dance, like crazy. Dovi, we're so blessed to count you as a friend. I know you have a lot of them. I follow you on Facebook.

I want to acknowledge one of our teachers for many years who is here today, Sue McGraw. She shared with me about you and it sums up our feelings: "[Dovi] is who he is. He always embraces life with joy and a big smile and asks, 'How are you?' He's one of the kindest people and brightest people I know in sharing sunlight. If you ever want a partner for ice cream, pizza, or a big smile, he's your man! He's our man and model for all of us on how to approach life with a smile always inside and out."

Why is Dovi on fire? Imagine if your nickname was Sunshine.

When we do a mitzvah, a good deed, or any transcendent act, and do so with spiritual intention, we access and realize the spiritual power of the act. We create the context and space for our souls to sing.

What happens in the soul when a person performs a mitzvah? A mitzvah is filled with divine inspirational force. As the Bible states, "These are the mitzvoth which a man shall do and live" (Leviticus 18:5). When we perform a soulful act, we receive a new dose of energy and life. A spiritual explosion occurs. Like a nuclear fusion of atoms, new life is released to the soul and to all of the worlds.

"The light of God of life, the light of the life of the world, lives in complete harmony with the glory of every mitzvah." In observance of a mitzvah, the soul meets with the light of God.

Because a soul is connected to the entire world, each seemingly small act, mitzvah, or act of kindness, is, in truth, a cosmic deed that fills the world with untold blessing. We possess the key to existence. When we perform a spiritual act, we open the valves of heavenly blessing and are refreshed and rejuvenated.

How do you feel when you help another human being? I'd venture to say that most of us feel good when we give of ourselves to others. Picking ourselves up and moving outside our comfort zone is not easy. We may be tired, busy, or oblivious. Perhaps we think someone else will do the good deed. Yet once we muster the energy to help another, we experience a feeling of accomplishment. When my children were younger, I'd tell them that when they did a mitzvah, their soul was smiling. It's the warm sensation we feel when we know we've done an act of significance.

We can't dictate emotions. I can't tell you to feel spiritual. It has to come from within. Judaism teaches a principle to awaken one's soul: actions effect emotions. If you don't feel like giving charitably, put your hand in your pocket and give charitably. Once you do, it'll become easier the next time because your soul will be more in tune with giving. Every mitzvah you do cracks the shell surrounding your soul and fuels the flame of the divine in you. Just as we work out and exercise to strengthen our muscles and increase our aerobic capacity, when we do a soulful act, we strengthen the spiritual muscles of our souls.

In fact, God reveals this secret in the book of Deuteronomy. The Bible states, "See, I place before you the choice of life and death, good and bad" (30:19). Rabbi Samson Raphael Hirsch explains that the Torah does not state the reward one receives for pursuing goodness because the reward is the act itself. The act generates a blessing within and deep joy. The act motivates us to continue to pursue more acts of goodness. In fact, the etymology of the word for *bracha*, blessing, is connected to the word for knees, indicating progress and growth. The knee is the power joint.

Choosing the path of life spurs us internally to reach for new spiritual heights. With all our emphasis on the health of our bodies, we may be neglecting our souls. Whether a believer or not, we all sense deep inside a yearning for meaning and significance in life. We seek purpose and to make an impact in the world. Our bodies may be whole, but our souls have a hole. Happiness in life stems from finding purpose.

> *"Behold, the days are coming," says*
> *the Lord God, "when I will send a famine*
> *into the land, not a famine for bread nor*
> *a thirst for water, but to hear*
> *the word of the Lord."*
>
> —Amos 8:11

We come into this world against our will. We depart against our will. God instills within every human being a homing device: his light. The light is our free choice, our pursuit of meaning in life, and our destiny. Many faith traditions possess rituals to solidify, sustain, and magnify that light. A baby naming service in Jewish tradition represents the moment when the soul is intrinsically linked to the body. The Hebrew name is our true identity.

Jewish mysticism teaches that parents are blessed with divine inspiration when choosing a name for a child. I remember Diane and I having in mind a name for one of our daughters, only to change our minds once we saw her at birth. It seemed in our souls the name was not right. We named our daughter Elisheva with this spirit in mind.

For many people, their Hebrew name is then used at another life-cycle event, perhaps a Bar or Bat Mitzvah or a wedding. This tradition extends across faiths. For instance, in Eastern Orthodoxy, during chrismation, a person is given a new name, usually one that reflects the soul of the person or the soul of a spiritual mentor such as a monk, matushka, or mystic. In many circles, this is the name that is used for that person from then on (instead of the name given at birth).

Yet ideally, it should be a touchstone for life. I'm about to tell you a secret. Mystics teach that your name reflects your soul. Hebrew letters for soul are *nun shin mem* and *heh*, and the two middle letters *men* and *shin* signify the word "name"; your name is the essence of your soul. Regardless of your faith tradition, learn about your name. What hopes and dreams were implanted in you at birth? Are you named after someone, a relative or a hero? Why?

Knowing our name and realizing its potential, and being guided by it, enables us to lead a soulful life. Our names are soul trackers. It's unfortunate when we may not remember our names and/or only use them at life-cycle events. Live by the names and our souls will shine.

In the final moments of our lives, it's not uncommon for us to hear our names summoned. When someone is sick, we use their name and that of their mother to pray to God on their behalf. As the soul transitions to a new dimension, mystics teach that God calls on the person by their Hebrew name. My father-in-law had such an experience. In his final days in the hospital in Charleston, South Carolina, hovering between life and death, he raised his hands above him as if he was being summoned and called out his name, Isaac, the son of Aryeh. It was an affirmation of another reality and the stirrings of his soul. It was an emanation of the ultimate summoning of our souls to the next world. Mystics teach that God calls on us at the end of our lives by our names to hold us accountable to our divine destiny.

When I was in Israel this past summer, I had the privilege of bestowing more than twenty names on college students who were visiting on a Birthright trip. No event is random, and I believe the moment was by design. Earlier in the week, I'd wandered into the office of Jeff Seidel, a man known for inviting people to the Western Wall for Friday night Sabbath experiences. His work is legendary. When I met him, he was wearing a suit and his trademark two-tone white and brown saddle shoes. It was the first time we'd met, and we immediately realized we were kindred spirits.

He asked me if I could help him on a Thursday night. His rabbi assistant was away, and he was asked to help a group of forty Birthright college students to become Bar or Bat Mitzvah at the wall. I came to Jerusalem to write, but I knew inside I couldn't pass up the mitzvah and opportunity. It was an unforgettable hour.

I spoke to them about my journey, why I'd chosen to be with them on that particular day, and the holiness of our time together. I asked how many of them knew how to optimize their smartphones, and I explained how important it was in life to learn how to optimize our souls. When they turned twelve or thirteen, they were then obligated in God's ways. However, this experience at the wall would be an opportunity to reconnect with who they were as Jews, as souls, and who they wanted to be. Most of the students had never been to

Israel, didn't have Hebrew names, and had never had a coming-of-age ceremony.

After sharing the significance of their Hebrew names, I either gave them one and/or if they had one shared the meaning and its relevance to their mission in life. They were so grateful, as was I for the opportunity to participate, and then I recited a prayer during which each person affirmed their Hebrew name. Then I gave them a blessing.

I closed by sharing the accounting at the end of life, when God calls our names, and I wished for each of them to realize their divine potential. I hoped that, with God's help, this moment would help build ongoing Jewish identity and inspire them toward leadership and realizing their soulful purpose in life.

Strategies

Meditate Every Day

Three times a day, I add a prayer that I hope to be the best conduit for God's blessings in the world. I'm a vessel. I'm here for God and not personal glory. The prayer is empowering. I acknowledge that I'm alive not for myself but to share some light with the world. My higher purpose is to be a blessing every day.

This idea crystallized in my mind when I graduated from high school. Like most teenagers, I asked my peers to autograph my year-book. I also asked one of my rabbis to sign it. He wrote a message that lives with me to this day. There is an obligation to love God. He asked, "How is it possible for God to dictate an emotion?" He quoted an idea from the Talmud that explains that our obligation in life is to act in a way that motivates others to see and bring Godliness in humanity and the world. I live to share my light. Although intellectually I knew this idea, it was only after a conversation with one of the great Jewish leaders of our time that this knowledge moved me every day.

I asked Rebbetzin Esther Jungreis about the key to her success. She shared her secret with me. She told me that every day she asks God to enable her to be the best blessing to the world that she can be. All of our talents and resources are here to amplify God's presence in the world.

Three times a day, I pray to God to be the conduit for that light, to fill me with his strength and spirit, to be a conduit for his glory in the world.

Tool Box

Allocate an hour for reflection on these existential questions and spiritual practice:

❶ What is your purpose?

❷ How are you a vessel for God or a higher purpose other than yourself?

❸ What talents do you possess and how can you use them to improve the life of another human being?

❹ Set a time every day to meditate or pray for strength and spirit to embrace your life purpose.

Love What You Do

> "*Choose a job you love, and you will never*
> *have to work a day in your life.*"
>
> —Author Unknown

We've all heard this phrase, but it serves as a reminder for one of the most effective ways to renew your energy every day. It reflects the anatomy of your soul. When your work reflects your innermost aspirations, your passion will be ignited. Not everyone is blessed to be in a profession that matches their life aspirations. Your job may be mundane from your perspective. However, never confuse your job with life or your mission with your purpose. No matter what you do, you'll find moments every day to make someone's day.

Recently, a friend of mine shared about his father, who worked for the department store Abraham and Strauss in the 1960s in New York City. He told me that his father would always go out of his way to say hello to the elevator men. It made an impression on him as a child and ignited within him the power of a simple hello. Within seconds, we can make someone smile and cheer them up. Second, don't underestimate the holiness of your work. You possess talents unique to you. Cultivate them and share your light. You are a diamond. Shine!

Take a Spiritual Inventory

Every month we receive a bank statement detailing the value of our financial accounts. Some of us watch the stock market every day or even hour by hour. We make decisions to buy, sell, or reinvest based on the information we receive. The value of your life is infinitely greater than any sum of money. Your life is a gift latent with infinite potential. Take a spiritual inventory to determine your assets and areas of investment with your time and talents. The profit you yield will be priceless.

Tool Box

❶ **Identify your talents:** work, home, and recreation.

❷ **Identify your skills.**

❸ **Smile factor:** What would you be willing to do for free; what makes you smile that requires little external motivation?

❹ **Reflect on these ideas;** find ways every day to harness them toward your life purpose.

I Am Alive When . . .

"If the sight of the blue skies fills you with joy, if a blade of grass springing up in the fields has power to move you, if the simple things of nature have a message that you understand, rejoice, for your soul is alive."

—Eleonora Duse

We measure our progress in miles per hour, calories lost. Measure your spiritual health in moments when you feel alive.

A couple of years ago, I had the good fortune to travel to Memphis for a rabbinic conference sponsored by Yeshiva University. Before arriving in Memphis, I was speaking with my father, and he said, "If you go to Memphis, you've got to visit Graceland." He said that if I didn't, it would be like going to Paris and not seeing the Louvre.

Upon arrival, a few hours before the conference began, a few of us colleagues decided to visit Graceland. I quickly learned that one colleague had absolutely no interest in going, but another one was a lifelong Elvis fan. The motto in Graceland is "Where Elvis still lives." It's true! We saw his albums, cars, movies—all Elvis, all the time.

When I returned home after the trip, I wanted to share the experience with my kids. I showed them a couple of videos of Elvis on YouTube. One of my kids said, "Is Elvis still alive?" I answered, "Well, it depends on who you ask."

I realized that while it may be true that for Elvis, the king, there is a question of whether he still lives, the King of Kings, the Almighty, lives forever. The real question is not whether God lives in the world but within us. Are we truly alive with the energy of a higher power or do we pass the days wondering how the time goes by?

Tool Box

Try a spiritual exercise. Compose a poem entitled, "I am alive when . . ." (fill in the phrase). When do you feel most alive? Find an hour to meditate on the question; write your poem and keep reading it weekly. Your vision will enable you to envision the practices that signify the very best you.

Here is mine:

I Am Alive When . . .

I am alive when I wake up every morning and recite the Modeh Ani.

I am alive when I sing.

I am alive when I sit with Diane and reflect on the day, even when I'm physically tired.

I am alive when I gaze into my children's eyes and truly "hear" them.

I am alive when I plumb the depths of Torah.

I am alive when I teach Torah, share my dreams, celebrate, and mourn with our congregation and strengthen our relationships.

I am alive when I walk through the woods or contemplate at the cove.

I am alive when I stand with Israel and Jews all over the world.

I am alive when I spread light to humanity and see the Godliness in every human being.

I am alive when I live Torah and love life.

I am alive when I maximize every moment of every day!

Answer the Call—Every Day

"There is no passion to be found playing small, in settling for a life that is less than the one you are capable of living."

—Nelson Mandela

"The sun has not caught me
in bed in fifty years."

—Thomas Jefferson

"The difference between rising at five
and seven o'clock in the morning, for forty years,
supposing a man to go to bed at the same hour
at night, is nearly equivalent to the addition
of ten years to a man's life."

—Phillip Doddridge

Good morning! A new day is a new lease on life. It's a call for each of us to seize the day to make a difference. Do you allow the days to fade away or harness every moment for impact? Motivation and energy flow when we view every day as an answer to a call.

When God asked Adam and Eve, "Where are you?" it was a call of intentionality and purpose. It's the difference between being a thermometer or a thermostat. Both register the temperature but one is influenced by the environment and the other transforms the environment. Are you a thermometer or a thermostat? Do you stay focused on shining light every day or do you get distracted? We're ultimately answerable to God and our inner spark and consciousness. Do we do our best every day?

In his book *The Call: Finding and Fulfilling the Central Purpose of Your Life*, Os Guinness writes that God planted a spiritual gyroscope deep inside our hearts. Every day we are called upon to be so enthralled with a vision of our Lord and God that "before others we have nothing to prove, nothing to gain, nothing whatsoever to lose."

"The Lord remains near to all who call out to him,
to everyone who calls out to him sincerely."

—Psalm 148:18

Tool Box

❶ Do you sense the wonder of being called? When?

❷ Do you sense that the calling is only for your benefit, your family, your community, or God?

❸ How do you answer the call every day?

❹ Stay focused through daily encounters with the Bible, Book of Wisdom, or a spiritual mentor.

When I walk in the streets, I see holiness. I see a world of souls who are striving and yearning for deep pleasure, enduring joy, and lives of eternal meaning and significance. I'm driven to do whatever I can with the gift of life to harness my divine potential to unlock these sparks. I'm no different from you. We're all conduits. There's so much more we can accomplish to lead the lives we want to lead. Answer the call. Rediscover your soul. Meditate daily. When we allow ourselves to be agents for a higher purpose in life, we'll be fortified in our mission with renewable energy every day of our lives!

Celebrity Stirrings

"We're on a mission from God."

—Elwood Blues, *The Blues Brothers*

Regardless of your faith tradition, the secret to staying motivated every day on your journey and inspiring others is by living life for a higher purpose. Two people who embody this ideal are Tamir Goodman and David Harris. Tamir Goodman, dubbed by *Sports Illustrated* as the "Jewish Jordan," who we met earlier in the book, is an American-born Israeli retired Orthodox Jewish basketball player. He intuitively understands the secret to discovering your renewable energy. "Basketball was given to me as a gift. I recognize that it is a tool to do as much good for the world as I can through the sport. I was always raised to ask myself, 'What does God want from me? What potential does he see in me?' I see every day as an opportunity to fulfill a holy mission to do my best and never rest."

David Harris, the executive director of AJC, who we also met earlier in the book, recognizes his role and all of ours in being the bridge between generations:

At a certain point in life, those who preceded us approach their own finish line. In a relay race, they're holding a baton that they need to transfer to someone else, if there is someone to receive the baton. Is the person who receives the baton willing to embrace it and then do his or her utmost to sprint during their own lap or laps, until they approach the finish line? The Jewish journey to me is very much the same. When you look at it mathematically, if we have a professional life span of forty years, and we're people, for argument's sake, four thousand years, then we're talking about 1 percent of the life journey of the Jewish people.

For those of us who believe in this journey, I think it's important that we view this as a relay race in which we do our utmost, in Olympic terms, to sprint as smartly, as swiftly, as intelligently as we can, but also to know in advance that there are people who are waiting at the end of my turn, my lap, who are prepared, willing, able, to receive the baton and to engage in their own swift, smart, intelligent sprint. That's the way I view it, so to me, leaving my organization will not just be about how many speeches I gave, or how many articles I wrote, though obviously for me, each one is important in its moment. It's more about structurally and spiritually what carries forward, both from me and beyond me.

I think what's particularly important is whether, at the end of the day, your legacy leaves when you leave. Whether there is something that you've built that outlasts you. And if it outlasts you, then it has to be about more than yourself. In other words, however satisfying a good speech, or a good op-ed, or a good meeting might be, unless there's something that outlasts you, which means is bigger than yourself, your legacy is likely to go with you, and I've seen it hundreds of times in organizations, including this one. So, for me, it's what outlasts me.

EPILOGUE

Each time a man stands up for an ideal,
or acts to improve the lot of others, or strikes out
against injustice, he sends forth a tiny ripple of
hope, and crossing each other from a million centers
of energy and daring those ripples build a current
which can sweep down the mightiest walls
of oppression and resistance.

—Robert F. Kennedy

What is your purpose in this world? We experience God when we emulate God. Darkness enveloped the world at the beginning of time. At the very beginning of time, God created the world with a burst of energy that gave birth to the planets, the stars, and then to life. Among all of the millions of forms of life, God created only one life-form in his image with the unique capacity to be his partner in creation. God endowed humanity, each of us, with the ability to choose between good and evil, harm and healing.

The world was born in darkness and chaos. God's first act was to create light and infuse morality, love, and holiness in the world. As God did, so shall we.

Your life is a candle. You are a flame. You can ignite thousands of lights in the world every day.

> *"There are two ways of spreading light:*
> *to be the candle or the mirror*
> *that reflects it."*
>
> —Edith Wharton

A story is told about a man who wished to bequeath his estate to one of his three sons. He offered the inheritance to the son who would best fill an empty room. One son chose bricks. Although they crowded the room, small, empty spaces remained. The second son filled the room with straw in an effort to fill even the smallest corners. The third son, not to be outdone by his brothers, brought his father into the empty and dark room. The father wondered what his son had in mind. The room was empty. His son, though, took out a candle and lit a flame. The room filled with light. When we lighten a dark world, we emulate God, and our souls will be on fire. When we make small differences in the world for one person, we align ourselves with life's purpose.

One of the great sages of the last century, Rabbi Yosef Elyashiv, died a couple of years ago at the age of 102. He delivered lectures to his students until six months before his passing. He requested no eulogies at his funeral. You might wonder if this was because people didn't know him or had little to say. In fact, 250,000 people attended his memorial service in the streets of Jerusalem and only Psalms were recited. Why no eulogies? It was remarked that for a man who lived his life every day to the fullest and was revered by so many both in life and death, no eulogies were necessary.

This is the goal. If we embody the principles of reverse engineering our lives, we'll live inspired to touch thousands of people and be known always for our very best selves.

The world is counting on you. Realize your divine potential.

At the end of our lives, we'll be shown two films. A heavenly usher escorts us into a movie theater. We think, "Wow! This is great. What are they showing up here?" We relax in a comfortable seat and eat popcorn. We learn it is a double feature. We ask, "What are they showing today? Is it *Lord of the Rings* in honor of God?" "No, there are two films today. One film is entitled, *How You Led Your Life*. The other film is entitled, *How You Could Have Led Your Life*." The difference between the two determines the amount of joy we'll experience now and forever.

Every day is your opportunity for spiritual greatness. Make every day a masterpiece. There is no person that is meant to do exactly what somebody else is meant to do. We are all unique. We are all created in God's image. All of us are born with the capacity to leave a mark on this world, to enrich our relationships now, and to lead a life of inspiration.

You have finished reading the book, but your journey is only beginning. You've read ideas and strategies to improve your life. You've encountered stories of motivation, strength, and hope. Reread the book until you've realized your aspirations. Although we may not have personally met, I feel we are kindred spirits. I opened my heart to you and I hope our souls have touched. We're all on a divine mission, and I hope we continue to grow in good health for many years. God believes in you.

Thank you for joining me on the journey to reverse engineer your life. We've only just begun. May God bless you and your loved ones, and may all of your most heartfelt desires come true.

NOTES

1 Karen Crouse, "Shades of Gray on Way to Podium," *New York Times* online, August 10, 2012, *http://www.nytimes.com/2012/08/11/sports /olympics/separating-the-person-from-the-olympic-performance .html?_r=0.*

2 Marc Angel, *Losing the Rat Race, Winning at Life* (Jerusalem: Urim Publications, 2005), 9–10.

3 Rabbi Moshe Hayyim Luzzatto, *The Path of the Just* (Spring Valley, NY: Feldheim, 2004), 8.

4 Mark Helprin, *A Soldier of the Great War* (Wilmington, MA: Mariner Books, 2005), 119.

5 This well-known story about Baron Rothschild may be found in numerous sources; see Rabbi Eliyahu Hoffmann, "Making One's Bed and Lying in It," *http://gt.torah.org/learning/olas-shabbos/5763/met zora.html?print=1*; Rabbi Shlomo Landau, "Baron Rothschild's Secret," *http://www.aish.com/ci/s/Baron-Rothschilds-Secret.html*; and "Wealth: It Depends What You Do with It," *Jewish History* blog, *http://www.jew ishhistory.org/wealth/.*

6 Shilo Rea, "Neurobiological Changes Explain How Mindfulness Meditation Improves Health," Carnegie Mellon University website, *http://www .cmu.edu/news/stories/archives/2016/february/meditation-changes -brain.html.*

7 Greg Doll, "Renewed by the Sabbath," Trinity Church, *http://trinity church.life/blog/renewed-by-the-sabbath.* This article first appeared in

the fall 2015 issue of *Trinity Life* magazine and is used here by permission of Greg Doll.

8 For a longer definition of each virtue in Franklin's understanding, see *http://www.thirteenvirtues.com/*.

9 Benjamin Franklin, *The Autobiography of Benjamin Franklin*, Electric Ben Franklin online, *http://www.ushistory.org/franklin/autobiography/page41.htm41*.

10 "Rags: A Story," from *The Language of Faith*, by Robert D. Dewey (United Church Press, 1963; new printing, 1967), 32–35. Used by permission.

11 The full speech is available at Nobelprize.org, *https://www.nobelprize.org/nobel_prizes/peace/laureates/1986/wiesel-acceptance_en.html*.

12 Michael Chapman, "Denzel Washington to College Grads: 'Put God First,'" CNSNews.com, *http://www.cnsnews.com/blog/michael-w-chapman/denzel-washington-college-grads-put-god-first*.

13 Lisa Miller, "Saved," *New York Magazine* online, *http://nymag.com/news/features/sports/mariano-rivera-2013-6/*.

14 Harav Yechiel Michel Tucazinsky, *Gesher Hachaim* (*The Bridge of Life*), 2nd ed. (Moznaim, 1983), 19.

ABOUT THE AUTHOR

Whether a mentor, guide, cheerleader, or motivator, Rabbi Daniel Cohen possesses a unique blend of authenticity, wisdom, and spiritual insight for contemporary society. His personal experience as a rabbi, sharing hundreds of life-affirming moments from birth to death and cultivating thousands of years of Jewish wisdom, and his experience as a husband and father of six daughters has provided him with a compelling narrative that he shares with humor and humanity.

Born and raised in Atlanta, Georgia, Rabbi Cohen is a graduate of Yeshiva University in New York and its Azrieli Graduate School. Rabbi Cohen began his career in West Orange, New Jersey, and has served in the rabbinate for more than twenty years. He currently serves as senior rabbi at Congregation Agudath Sholom in Stamford, Connecticut, the largest modern orthodox synagogue in New England.

Rabbi Cohen frequently speaks on leading a life of legacy. He also cohosts the nationally syndicated radio show *The Rabbi and the Reverend* with Reverend Greg Doll on the Gab Radio Network. He enjoys doing magic shows, playing sports, writing, searching for God, and living life with joy and an ever-present smile! Rabbi Cohen and his wife Diane are the grateful parents of six daughters. For more information about Rabbi Cohen, visit *www.rabbidanielcohen.com.*